A Catechism and Confession of Faith

BY ROBERT BARCLAY

A new edition
edited in modern English by
Dean Freiday and Arthur O. Roberts

BARCLAY PRESS
Newberg, OR 97132

A CATECHISM AND CONFESSION OF FAITH

© 2001 by Dean Freiday and Arthur O. Roberts

Published by
BARCLAY PRESS
211 N. Meridian Street, #101
Newberg, Oregon, 97132
800.962.4014
www.barclaypress.com

ISBN 978-1-59498-017-6

All rights reserved.
No part may be reproduced by any method for any purpose without permission in writing from the copyright holders, except brief quotation in connection with a literary review.

Scripture quotations are from the New Revised Standard Version of the Bible, copyright 1989 by the Division of Christian Education of the National Council of the Churches of Christ in the USA. Used by permission. All rights reserved.

Table of Contents

Foreword	by Paul Anderson	v
Preface	by Robert Barclay	xi
Chapter One	Of the True and Saving Knowledge of God	1
Chapter Two	The Rule and Guide of Christians, and of the Scriptures	3
Chapter Three	The Significance of Jesus Christ Manifest in the Flesh	7
Chapter Four	The New Birth, the Inward Presence of Christ and the Unity of Believers	15
Chapter Five	The Light by which Christ Enlightens Everyone: The Universality and Sufficiency of God's Grace	21
Chapter Six	Faith, Justification, and Works	33
Chapter Seven	Perfection, or Freedom from Sin	39
Chapter Eight	Perseverance and Falling from Grace	47
Chapter Nine	The Church and Ministry	51
Chapter Ten	Worship	63

Chapter Eleven	Baptism, Bread and Wine	67
Chapter Twelve	The Life of a Christian	73
Chapter Thirteen	Governance	89
Chapter Fourteen	The Resurrection	93
Chapter Fifteen	A Short Introduction to the Confession of Faith	95
Chapter Sixteen	A Confession of Faith, in 23 Articles	97
Chapter Seventeen	A Short Discussion and Appeal to All Christians	111
Chapter Eighteen	A Brief Look at Scriptural Proofs of Selected Articles in the Westminster Confession of Faith	115
Appendix A	Barclay's original title page	121
Appendix B	Editorial notes about method and text	123

Foreword

Robert Barclay is most widely known for writing the *Apology for the True Christian Divinity* (1676 in Latin; 1678 in English). But this was not his first important Quaker work. *A Catechism and Confession of Faith* was written in 1673, about seven years after his "convincement" of the truth, and when he was only 24 years old.

In his preface to the *Catechism* he writes that he envisioned early on that such a piece would be both possible and feasible. How right he was! Much of the scriptural foundation for the propositions in the *Apology* are clearly laid out in this important work. While the *Apology* argues Quaker assertions theologically, and within the realm of philosophic rational discourse, the *Catechism and Confession of Faith* is designed to walk the common reader into the spiritual faith and vital religious experience at the heart of early Christianity.

The editors and I believe that making it available again in this accessible form will not only provide Friends a useful tool for religious educators to use, but it will also magnify the center of "basic Christianity" in ways that could make a difference in the larger world.

Set against the backdrop of the Westminster Confession, the *Catechism and Confession of Faith* claims continuity with the Reformers in adhering to the authoritative teachings of the scriptures and the goal of recovering the heart of Apostolic Christianity. Critically engaging the various expressions of established religion, Barclay shows himself to be a religious sociologist ahead of his time as well as an astute biblical theologian. He criticizes not simply one group or another but points to the tendency of all religious organizations to "depart from the simple, pure gospel that had been delivered in its original splendor and integrity." In this sense, Barclay sought to continue the reform begun by Luther and others by seeking *to reform the Reformation*, appealing to its original aspirations and callings, lest their successors establish and build up "what their fathers pulled down!"

While not all of these "accretions" resulted from "yielding to the inclinations of the ego," Barclay effectively turns the Reformers' criticisms of Catholicism against the Protestants' own "substitutes for the gospel" and tendencies to exalt opinions and notions "above the truth"—particularly as revealed in scripture. At this point, Barclay constructs his outline of the

Christian faith upon the two foundational premises of the Reformation itself: that scripture should be held as the authoritative measure of all principles and doctrines, and that the plain and easily understood meanings of scripture are to be preferred over more convoluted ones. Barclay therefore constructs his approaches to central Christian doctrines in a question-and-answer format highlighting the teachings of scripture in response to questions of the day.

This approach was designed to provide instruction regarding the central teachings of scripture, but it also served an apologetic function. It defended Quakers against the accusations of some Protestant leaders that their views were either unorthodox or unscriptural. Barclay here points out the irony that those who claimed to reform the Christian faith on the basis of scripture were now persecuting a group whose principles "are found in scripture, word for word!" Here is a case where the basic Quaker faith is presented not as new revelation challenging scripture, but scriptural doctrine challenging the conjectures of those claiming to be biblical authorities, but who had denied central motifs within scripture: including the clear teachings of Jesus, the saving and sanctifying work of Christ, the authentic character of worship and ministry, and the ongoing leadership of the risen Christ through the work of the Holy Spirit. The appeal to the reader is put in most inviting terms:

> If you really love the scriptures and desire to hold the plain doctrines derived from them, rather than to far-fetched implications, you will easily observe there the complete principles of the people called Quakers. These views are clearly couched in scripture words, without addition or commentary, particularly in respect to what adversaries claim against them. On controversial matters the scriptures plainly decide. No quibbling, no academic subtleties (or worldly wisdom) that multiply words without adding knowledge and only obscure the meaning....
>
> I shall leave it to the rational judgment of readers unbiased by self-interest (that great enemy of fairness) and willing to follow the light of Christ in their conscience to decide if the scriptures do not pertinently and aptly answer the questions!

Barclay's next move is a brilliant one. Rather than assert a confession and then back it up by scripture, he begins with the scriptural content first. Only after the light of scripture has been cast upon fourteen topics central to the Christian faith does Barclay introduce the fifteenth and sixteenth chapters, which involve a Confession of Faith and its introduction. An interesting fact about the topics covered in the Confession of Faith is that nearly all of its articles relate to the authenticity of religious experience and its implications. From the immediacy of experiencing God to the possibility of perfection and sanctification, Barclay challenges the ways Protestants and others either lowered their standards for the normal Christian life or delimited its attainment to organizational means.

This is followed, however, by "A Short Discussion and Appeal to All Christians" (Chapter Seventeen) in which Barclay criticizes Roman Catholics for depending too heavily upon tradition rather than scripture, Socinians for denying the divinity of Christ, Arminians for not grounding optimism in "that spiritual force that enlightens everyone—the Light of Christ," and finally the Protestants again for their refusal to heed the very scriptures they claimed with such vehemence to be authoritative. He challenges their teaching that God has "committed his counsel wholly to writing" by citing clear scriptures which emphasize the ongoing revelatory work of Christ. Likewise, Barclay challenges wooden approaches to the Sabbath and unscriptural developments of the sacraments. Barclay chose these issues at least in part because Friends had been persecuted for not living up to Protestant doctrines, and yet Barclay exposes with ample clarity the weak scriptural bases of these dogmatic views.

The appendices and comments by Dean Freiday at the end of the volume shed valuable light on Barclay's work, including issues related to the producing of a critical text. Arthur Roberts likewise has added notes and applied his keen critical mind to many of the issues involved in producing this book. The use of the NRSV is important to the work, even though Barclay worked from the 1611 Authorized Version. The text-critical discoveries made over the last century and the overall adequacy of the NRSV translation serve Barclay's work well, and notes have been added when the reference to the earlier version, or other modern translations seems helpful. The teamwork of Arthur Roberts and Dean Freiday makes a winning combination here, and the world is indebted to their labor and astute judgment in preparing this reader-friendly text.

How will Barclay's *Catechism and Confession of Faith* be used? Only time will tell. For one thing, it makes an excellent discussion resource and study guide for young people and adults alike seeking to be deepened in Quaker beliefs and perspectives. However, lest it be assumed that such a piece will be of value only to the family of Friends, it is my belief that the broader world will be challenged and inspired by this important volume as well. It will certainly instruct many about the character of early Quaker faith and practice, but more importantly, it will help all of us consider more carefully the character of authentic Christian faith and expression. After all, such is the central Quaker vocation.

> Paul Anderson
> *professor of biblical and Quaker studies*
> *George Fox University*

A CATECHISM
AND
CONFESSION OF FAITH

FAITHFUL TO THE BELIEFS
OF THE CHURCHES OF CHRIST
CALLED QUAKER AND
CONSISTENT WITH EARLY CHRISTIANITY
AS DEMONSTRATED
THROUGH THE SCRIPTURES

BY ROBERT BARCLAY

FIRST PUBLISHED IN 1673

A new edition
edited in modern English by
Dean Freiday and Arthur O. Roberts

*You search the scriptures because you think that in them
you have eternal life; and it is they that testify on my behalf.
Yet you refuse to come to me to have life.*
John 5:39-40

Barclay's Catechism and Confession of Faith

Preface

Apostasy began in the hearts and minds of people who, even in the apostles' days, began to depart from the simple, pure gospel that had been delivered in its original splendor and integrity.

Innumerable notions and opinions have arisen from yielding to the inclinations of the ego. Such accretions have burdened the Christian faith, first by adding new ideas and then by exalting them above the truth. In time, then, these additions became substitutes for the gospel and eventually truth came to be shut out, while religiosity took its place under the name Christian; but it wasn't the real thing.

Fortunately, it pleased God in nearly every age and generation to raise up witnesses to bear testimony to truth and against superstition and apostasy. This was especially true in Germany in the 16th century, where light broke forth and spread to many other nations. Indeed, the "beast" received a deadly wound! Many people at one time or another protested against and left the church of Rome, rejecting accumulated traditions and rituals verging on the superstitious.[1]

But alas! Lamentably the successors of these Protestants are establishing and building up what their fathers pulled down! Obviously, they did not continue with the honorable work of reformation. Although broken into factions, Protestants generally agree in distancing themselves from the Roman Catholic Church on two issues.

First, every principle and doctrine of the Christian faith is, and ought to be, founded upon the scriptures. Whatever principles and doctrines that are contrary to or not supported by the scriptures ought to be rejected.

---

[1] Christian dialogue in the 17th century tended toward pejorative terminology in reference to other Christians. Despite Quaker criticism of Roman Catholicism, there were fraternal contacts. William Penn's godfather was Charles II. When two Quaker women were imprisoned on Malta by the Inquisition, George Fox appealed, successfully, to the Catholic royal almoner. And Gulielma Penn visited Charles II when he was exiled on the Continent.

Second, the scriptures themselves are plain and easily understood; and Christians—individually and as church members—ought to read and study them. Their faith and belief should be founded upon them. They should receive them for that reason alone, and not because a church or assembly has issued a recommendation of them. Even the best and purest church pronouncements can be fallible.

Despite such acknowledged principles, these Protestants vigorously prosecute and persecute others as severely as the Catholics did their fathers. Why? For believing things plainly set forth in the scriptures, and for refusing to believe traditions not founded upon them. To detail these abuses would enlarge this preface beyond proper bounds, so I have allotted a chapter to the subject.

Regretfully, I notice these Protestant leaders act like the scribes and Pharisees of old, who exalted Moses and the prophets, and boasted proudly of being Abraham's children. And yet these scribes and Pharisees were the greatest opposers and vilifiers of Christ, to whom Moses and the prophets gave witness. Indeed, they accused Christ of being a lawbreaker and a blasphemer. Isn't this an ironic parallel: there is now a people greatly persecuted and bitterly reviled, accused as heretics, by a generation that proclaims and exalts the scriptures? And yet the principles of this persecuted group are found in scripture, word for word! Nevertheless the grossest slander cast upon these people is that they vilify and deny the scriptures and replace them with their own conjectures.

This *Catechism and Confession of Faith* is compiled and presented to you, as an impartial reader, in order to disprove such allegations. If you really love the scriptures and desire to hold the plain doctrines derived from them, rather than to far-fetched implications, you will easily observe there the complete principles of the people called Quakers. These views are clearly couched in scripture words, without addition or commentary, particularly in respect to what adversaries claim against them. On controversial matters the scriptures plainly decide. No quibbling, no academic subtleties (or worldly wisdom) that multiply words without adding knowledge and only obscure the meaning. In the answers to questions, not one word has been added, that I know of, to the express words of scripture. If in some of the questions my comments have been added to the plain and naked meaning of the words, this was done to make the meaning clearer, not to impose my judgment upon the reader. In some cases words have been added to provide a clear transition to the next question.

I shall leave it to the rational judgment of readers unbiased by self-interest (that great enemy of fairness) and willing to follow the light of Christ in their consciences to decide if the scriptures do not pertinently and aptly answer the questions!

I have deliberately, and with good reasons, deviated from the order followed by most confessions and catechisms hitherto published....Usually the confession of faith is placed before the catechism. I think it should be otherwise. What is composed for young people or other persons less informed, ought in my mind be placed first. It is more orderly to begin with easier and more readily understood things and then progress to those that are more difficult and involved. Besides, the questions included in the catechism, along with various objections answered there, will enable the reader better to understand the confession, which consists mostly of positive assertions.

Shortly after I received and believed the testimony I now share, I envisioned both the possibility and the usefulness of such a work. Now, after a fuller acquaintance with the holy scriptures, I have found time to accomplish it.

No doubt this work could be improved by additional citations, which are here omitted as not being immediately recalled. But I am content. God has assisted me thus far in his work by his Spirit, the good "remembrancer." I hope that as a result of this work serious and conscientious people will be helped to find and hold to the truth, and that it will sustain and confirm those who already believe. This I earnestly desire and pray for.

ROBERT BARCLAY
a servant of the church of Christ

From Urie, where I live; in my native country of Scotland,
the 11th of the sixth month, 1673 [August old style].

[Ed. Note. Robert Barclay was born December 23, 1648;
he died October 3, 1690]

Chapter One

Of the True and Saving Knowledge of God

1. Q. Christians of all kinds agree that the highest happiness consists in coming to know and to enjoy eternal life; what is Christ's understanding and judgment about it?

   A. *John 17:3.* And this is eternal life, that they may know you, the only true God, and Jesus Christ whom you have sent.

2. Q. How does God reveal this knowledge?

   A. *2 Cor. 4:6.* For it is the God who said, "Let light shine out of darkness," who has shone in our hearts to give the light of the knowledge of the glory of God in the face of Jesus Christ.

3. Q. How many Gods are there?

   A. *Eph. 4:6.* One God.

   1 Cor. 8:4, 6. There is one God, the Father, from whom are all things and for whom we exist, and one Lord, Jesus Christ, through whom are all things and through whom we exist.

4. Q. What is God?

   A. *John 4:24.* God is spirit.

5. Q. Among all the wonderful attributes of God found in the scriptures, which is most important for us, the closest to the apostolic Gospel witness?

   A. *1 John 1:5.* This is the message we have heard from him and proclaim to you, that God is light and in him there is no darkness at all.

6. Q. Who bears record in heaven to this message?

A. *1 John 5:7.* There are three that testify: the Father, the Word, and the Holy Spirit, and these three agree.[2]

7. Q. How does anyone come to know God the Father, according to Christ's words?

A. *Luke 10:22.* See also Matt. 11:27. All things have been handed over to me by my Father; and no one knows who the Son is except the Father, or who the Father is except the Son and anyone to whom the Son chooses to reveal him.

John 14:6. Jesus said to him, "I am the way, and the truth, and the life. No one comes to the Father except through me."

8. Q. By whom, and in what way, does the Son reveal this knowledge?

A. *1 Cor. 2:9-12.* But, as it is written, "What no eye has seen, nor ear heard, nor the human heart conceived, what God has prepared for those who love him"— these things God has revealed to us through the Spirit; for the Spirit searches everything, even the depths of God. For what human being knows what is truly human except the human spirit that is within? So also no one comprehends what is truly God's except the Spirit of God. Now we have received not the spirit of the world, but the Spirit that is from God, so that we may understand the gifts bestowed on us by God.[3]

John 14:26. But the Advocate, the Holy Spirit, whom the Father will send in my name, will teach you everything, and remind you of all that I have said to you.

---

[2] This is from the New King James Version. The New Revised Standard and other versions have deleted this verse because it does not appear in the earliest manuscripts. Consequently in them verse 7 reads what in the King James Version is verse 8: "And there are three that bear witness on earth: the Spirit, the water, and the blood, and these three agree as one."

[3] In the Contemporary English Version, American Bible Society (hereafter CEV), the text reads: But it is just as the Scriptures say, "What God has planned for people who love him is more than eyes have seen or ears have heard. It has never even entered our minds! God's Spirit has shown you everything. His Spirit finds out everything, even what is deep in the mind of God. You are the only one who knows what is in your own mind, and God's Spirit is the only one who knows what is in God's mind. But God has given us his Spirit. That's why we don't think the same way that the people of this world think. That's also why we can recognize the blessings that God has given us."

Chapter Two

The Rule and Guide of Christians, and of the Scriptures

1 Q. Because it is by the Spirit that Christ reveals the knowledge of God in things spiritual, is it by this Spirit that we must be led under the Gospel?

    A. *Rom. 8:9, 14.* But you are not in the flesh; you are in the Spirit, since the Spirit of God dwells in you. Anyone who does not have the Spirit of Christ does not belong to him….For all who are led by the Spirit of God are children of God.[4]

2 Q. Is this inward principle, then, the guide and rule for Christians?

    A. *1 John 2:27.* As for you, the anointing that you received from him abides in you, and so you do not need anyone to teach you. But as his anointing teaches you about all things, and is true and is not a lie, and just as it has taught you, abide in him.[5]

    1 Thess. 4:9. Now concerning love of the brothers and sisters, you do not need to have anyone write to you, for you yourselves have been taught by God to love one another.

---

[4] CEV: You are no longer ruled by your desires, but by God's Spirit, who lives in you. People who don't have the Spirit of Christ in them don't belong to him….Only those people who are led by God's Spirit are his children.

[5] The Revised English Bible (hereafter REB) reads: But as for you, the anointing which you received from him remains with you; you need no other teacher, but you learn all you need to know from his anointing, which is true and no lie. Dwell in him as he taught you to do.

Q. If Christians are to be taught by an inward anointing, is this principle at the very heart of the new covenant era?

A. *Hebr. 8:10-11.* This is the covenant that I will make with the house of Israel after those days, says the Lord: I will put my laws in their minds, and write them on their hearts, and I will be their God, and they shall be my people. And they shall not teach one another or say to each other, "Know the Lord," for they shall all know me, from the least of them to the greatest.

John 6:45. [It is written in the prophets], "And they shall all be taught by God."

 Q. Did Christ, therefore, promise that the Spirit should both abide with his disciples, and be in them?

A. *John 14:16-17.* And I will ask the Father, and he will give you another Advocate, to be with you forever. This is the Spirit of truth, whom the world cannot receive, because it neither sees him nor knows him. You know him, because he abides with you, and he will be in you.

 Q. Why were these scriptures written?

A. *Rom. 15:4.* For whatever was written in former days was written for our instruction, so that by steadfastness and by the encouragement of the scriptures we might have hope.[6]

6️⃣ Q. How are they useful?

A. *2 Tim. 3:15-17.* ...from childhood you have known the sacred writings that are able to instruct you for salvation through faith in Christ Jesus. All scripture is inspired by God and is useful for teaching, for reproof, for correction, and for training in righteousness, so that everyone who belongs to God may be proficient, equipped for every good work.[7]

---

[6] TEV (Good News Bible, or Today's English): Everything written in the Scriptures was written to teach us, in order that we might have hope through the patience and encouragement the Scriptures give us.

[7] TEV: ...and you remember that ever since you were a child you have known the Holy Scriptures, which are able to give you the wisdom that leads to salvation through faith in Christ Jesus. All Scripture is inspired by God and is useful for teaching the truth, rebuking error, correcting faults, and giving instruction for right living, so that the man who serves God may be fully qualified and equipped to do every kind of good work.

(7) Q. What gives the scriptures their preeminence?

A. *2 Pet. 1:20-21.* First of all you must understand this, that no prophecy of scripture is a matter of one's own interpretation, because no prophecy ever came by human will, but men and women moved by the Holy Spirit spoke from God.

(8) Q. If the scriptures are trustworthy because Spirit given, and because they testify that the Spirit will lead us into all truth, what did Christ mean when he commanded us to search them?

A. *John 5:39.* You search the scriptures because you think that in them you have eternal life; and it is they that testify on my behalf....[8]

(9) Q. I understand that in old times some people exalted the scriptures and yet would not believe them, nor allow themselves to be guided by them. How does Christ speak to this?

A. *John 5:45-47.* Do not think that I will accuse you before the Father; your accuser is Moses, on whom you have set your hope. If you believed Moses, you would believe me, for he wrote about me. But if you do not believe what he wrote, how will you believe what I say?[9]

(10) Q. How do we account for folks who claim to be ruled by, but do not obey, the scriptures?

A. *2 Pet. 3:16.* ...speaking of this as he [Paul] does in all his letters. There are some things in them hard to understand, which the ignorant and unstable twist to their own destruction, as they do the other scriptures.

---

[8] REB: You study the scriptures diligently, supposing that in having them you have eternal life; their testimony points to me.

[9] The NIV (New International Version) reads: But do not think I will accuse you before the Father. Your accuser is Moses, on whom your hopes are set. If you believed Moses, you would believe me, for he wrote about me. But since you do not believe what he wrote, how are you going to believe what I say?

Chapter Three

The Significance of Jesus Christ Manifest in the Flesh

1 Q. Which scriptures most obviously prophesy Christ's coming?

A. *Deut. 18:15.* The Lord your God will raise up for you a prophet like me from among your own people; you shall heed such a prophet.

Isa. 7:14. Therefore the Lord himself will give you a sign. Look, the young woman is with child and shall bear a son, and shall name him Immanuel.

2 Q. Was not Jesus Christ real before appearing in human form? What scriptures prove this against those who erroneously assert the contrary?

A. *Micah 5:2.* But you, O Bethlehem of Ephrathah, who are one of the little clans of Judah, from you shall come forth for me one who is to rule in Israel, whose origin is from of old, from ancient days.

John 1:1-3. In the beginning was the Word, and the Word was with God, and the Word was God. He was in the beginning with God. All things came into being through him, and without him not one thing came into being.[10]

John 8:58. Jesus said to them, "Very truly, I tell you, before Abraham was, I am."

John 17:5. So now, Father, glorify me in your own presence with the glory that I had in your presence before the world existed.

Eph. 3:9. …to make everyone see what is the plan of the mystery hidden for ages in God who created all things.

---

[10] REB: In the beginning the Word already was. The Word was in God's presence, and God was, the Word was. He was with God at the beginning, and through him all things came to be; without him no created thing came into being.

Col. 1:16. ...for in him all things in heaven and on earth were created, things visible and invisible, whether thrones or dominions or rulers or powers—all things have been created through him and for him.[11]

Hebr. 1:2. ...but in these last days he has spoken to us by a Son, whom he appointed heir of all things, through whom he also created the worlds.[12]

Q. These show clearly that even the world was created by Christ. But what scriptures prove the divinity of Christ against those who falsely deny it?

A. *John 1:1.* ...and the Word was God.

Rom. 9:5. ...to them belong the patriarchs, and from them, according to the flesh, comes the Messiah, who is over all, God blessed forever. Amen.

Phil. 2:6. ...who, though he was in the form of God, [Jesus] did not regard equality with God as something to be exploited.

1 John 5:20. And we know that the Son of God has come and has given us understanding so that we may know him who is true; and we are in him who is true, in his Son Jesus Christ. He is the true God and eternal life.[13]

Q. What glorious names do the scriptures give to Jesus Christ, the eternal son of God?

A. *Isa. 9:6.* He is named Wonderful Counselor, Mighty God, Everlasting Father, Prince of Peace.

Col. 1:15. He is the image of the invisible God, the firstborn of all creation.

---

[11] CEV: Everything was created by him, everything in heaven and on earth, everything seen and unseen, including all forces and powers, and all rulers and authorities. All things were created by God's Son, and everything was made for him.

[12] CEV: But now at last, God sent his Son to bring his message to us. God created the universe by his Son, and everything will someday belong to the Son.

[13] CEV: We know that Jesus Christ the Son of God has come and has shown us the true God. And because of Jesus, we now belong to the true God who gives eternal life.

Hebr. 1:3a. He is the reflection of God's glory and the exact imprint of God's very being.[14]

Rev. 19:13. He is clothed in a robe dipped in blood, and his name is called The Word of God.

5 Q. How did Jesus' birth come about?

A. *Matt. 1:18.* Now the birth of Jesus the Messiah took place in this way. When his mother Mary had been engaged to Joseph, but before they lived together, she was found to be with child from the Holy Spirit.

Luke 1:30-35. The angel said to her, "Do not be afraid, Mary, for you have found favor with God. And now, you will conceive in your womb and bear a son, and you will name him Jesus. He will be great, and will be called the Son of the Most High, and the Lord God will give to him the throne of his ancestor David." ...Mary said to the angel, "How can this be, since I am a virgin?" The angel said to her, "The Holy Spirit will come upon you, and the power of the Most High will overshadow you; therefore the child to be born will be holy; he will be called Son of God."

6 Q. Was Jesus Christ, born of the virgin Mary, and assumed to be the son of Joseph, an actual, real person?

A. *Hebr. 2:14, 16, 17.* Since, therefore, the children share flesh and blood, he himself likewise shared the same things, so that through death he might destroy the one who has the power of death, that is, the devil....For it is clear that he did not come to help angels, but the descendants of Abraham. Therefore he had to become like his brothers and sisters in every respect, so that he might be a merciful and faithful high priest in the service of God, to make a sacrifice of atonement for the sins of the people.

Hebr. 4:15. For we do not have a high priest who is unable to sympathize with our weaknesses, but we have one who in every respect has been tested as we are, yet without sin.[15]

---

[14] CEV: God's Son all the brightness of God's own glory and is like him in every way. [Barclay adds this footnote in his 1690 edition: "or more properly, according to the Greek, 'of his *substance.*'"]

[15] CEV: Jesus understands every weakness of ours, because he was tempted in every way that we are. But he did not sin!

Rom. 5:15. ...and the free gift in the grace of the one man, Jesus Christ, abounded for the many.

1 Cor. 15:20-21. But in fact Christ has been raised from the dead, the first fruits of those who have died. For since death came through a human being, the resurrection of the dead has also come through a human being.

7 Q. How do scriptures assert the conjunction and unity of God's eternal Son in and with the human person, Christ Jesus?

A. *John 1:14.* And the Word became flesh and lived among us, and we have seen his glory, the glory as of a father's only son, full of grace and truth.[16]

John 3:34. He whom God has sent speaks the words of God, for he gives [to Christ] the Spirit without measure.

Acts 10:38. ...how God anointed Jesus of Nazareth with the Holy Spirit and with power; how he went about doing good and healing all who were oppressed by the devil, for God was with him.

Col. 1:19. For in him all the fullness of God was pleased to dwell,[17]

Col. 2:9. For in him the whole fullness of deity dwells bodily,

Col. 2:3. ...in whom are hidden all the treasures of wisdom and knowledge.[18]

8 Q. For what purpose did Christ come into the world?

A. *Rom. 8:3.* For God has done what the law, weakened by the flesh, could not do: by sending his own Son in the likeness of sinful flesh, and to deal with sin, he condemned sin in the flesh,[19]

1 John 3:8, 5. Everyone who commits sin is a child of the devil; for the devil has been sinning from the beginning. The Son of God was revealed for this purpose, to destroy the works of the devil....You know that he was revealed to take away sins, [and in him there is no sin].

---

[16] CEV: The Word became a human being and lived here with us. We saw his true glory, the glory of the only Son of the Father. From him all the kindness and all the truth of God have come down to us.

[17] CEV: God himself was pleased to live fully in his Son.

[18] TEV: ...but all his wisdom and knowledge are hidden away in him.

[19] TEV: The Law of Moses cannot do this, because our selfish desires make the Law weak. But God set you free when he sent his own Son to be like us sinners and to be a sacrifice for our sin. God used Christ's body to condemn sin.

9 Q. Was Jesus really crucified and raised again?

A. *1 Cor. 15:3-4.* For I handed on to you as of first importance what I in turn had received: that Christ died for our sins in accordance with the scriptures, and that he was buried, and that he was raised on the third day in accordance with the scriptures.[20]

10 Q. What was the purpose of Christ's birth, death, and sufferings?

A. *Luke 2:30-32.* ...my eyes have seen your salvation, which you have prepared in the presence of all peoples, a light for revelation to the Gentiles and for glory to your people Israel.

Rom. 3:25. ...whom God put forward as a sacrifice of atonement by his blood, effective through faith. He did this to show his righteousness, because in his divine forbearance he had passed over the sins previously committed.[21]

Eph. 5:2. ...live in love, as Christ loved us and gave himself up for us, a fragrant offering and sacrifice to God.[22]

Col. 1:20-22. ...through him God was pleased to reconcile to himself all things, whether on earth or in heaven, by making peace through the blood of his cross. And you who were once estranged and hostile in mind, doing evil deeds, he has now reconciled in his fleshly body through death, so as to present you holy and blameless and irreproachable before him.[23]

---

[20] The Living Bible reads: I passed on to you right from the first what had been told to me, that Christ died for our sins according to the Scriptures. And that he was buried, and that three days afterwards he arose from the grave just as the prophets foretold.

[21] The New Jerusalem Bible (NJerB): God appointed him as a sacrifice for reconciliation, through faith, by the shedding of his blood, and so showed his justness: first for the past, when sins went unpunished because he held his hand.

[22] CEV: Let love be your guide. Christ loved us and offered his life for us as a sacrifice that pleases God.

[23] CEV: And God was pleased for him to make peace by sacrificing his blood on the cross, so that all beings in heaven and on earth would be brought back to God. You used to be far from God. Your thoughts made you his enemies, and you did evil things. But his Son became a human and died. So God made peace with you, and now he lets you stand in his presence as people who are holy and faultless and innocent.

Hebr. 9:12, 14. He entered once for all into the Holy Place, not with the blood of goats and calves, but with his own blood, thus obtaining eternal redemption. How much more will the blood of Christ, who through the eternal Spirit offered himself without blemish to God, purify our conscience from dead works to worship the living God!

1 Pet. 3:18. For Christ also suffered for sins once for all, the righteous for the unrighteous, in order to bring you to God. He was put to death in the flesh, but made alive in the spirit,[24]

1 John 3:16. We know love by this, that he laid down his life for us.

Hebr. 9:15. For this reason he is the mediator of a new covenant, so that those who are called may receive the promised eternal inheritance.

11 Q. Is Christ, then, the mediator?

A. *1 Tim. 2:5, 6.* For there is one God; there is also one mediator between God and humankind, Christ Jesus, himself human, who gave himself a ransom for all—this was attested at the right time.

12 Q. Was Christ the mediator before his earthly appearance and crucifixion?

A. *Rev. 5:12 and 13:8.* Worthy is the Lamb that was slaughtered....from the foundation of the world....

13 Q. Is it essential, then, to believe that the saints of old did partake of Christ, as one present with and nourishing them?

A. *1 Cor. 10:1-4.* I do not want you to be unaware, brothers and sisters, that our ancestors were all under the cloud, and all passed through the sea, and all were baptized into Moses in the cloud and in the sea, and all ate the same spiritual food, and all drank the same spiritual drink. For they drank from the spiritual rock that followed them, and the rock was Christ.[25]

---

[24] NJerB: Christ himself died once and for all for sins, the upright for the sake of the guilty, to lead us to God. In the body he was put to death, in the spirit he was raised to life.

[25] CEV: Friends, I want to remind you that all of our ancestors walked under the cloud and went through the sea. This was like being baptized and becoming followers of Moses. All of them ate the same spiritual food and drank the same spiritual drink, which flowed from the spiritual rock that followed them. That rock was Christ.

14 Q. The scriptures cited generally indicate that the sufferings and death of Christ are effective for destroying, removing, and pardoning sin; did he accomplish this while outwardly on the earth, or did he leave something for himself to do in us, and for us to do in and by his strength?

A. *1 Pet. 2:21.* For to this you have been called, because Christ also suffered for you, leaving you an example, so that you should follow in his steps....

Col. 1:23-24. I, Paul, became a servant of this gospel. I am now rejoicing in my sufferings for your sake, and in my flesh I am completing what is lacking in Christ's afflictions for the sake of his body, that is, the church.

2 Cor. 4:10-11. ...always carrying in the body the death of Jesus, so that the life of Jesus may also be made visible in our bodies. For while we live, we are always being given up to death for Jesus' sake, so that the life of Jesus may be made visible in our mortal flesh.[26]

2 Cor. 5:15. And he died for all, so that those who live might live no longer for themselves, but for him who died and was raised for them.[27]

Phil. 3:10. I want to know Christ and the power of his resurrection and the sharing of his sufferings by becoming like him in his death....

---

[26] TEV: At all times we carry in our mortal bodies the death of Jesus, so that his life also may be seen in our bodies. Throughout our lives we are always in danger of death for Jesus' sake, in order that his life may be seen in this mortal body of ours.

[27] New American Bible (NAB) reads: He indeed died for all, so that those who live might no longer live for themselves but for him who for their sake died and was raised.

Chapter Four

The New Birth, the Inward Presence of Christ, and the Unity of Believers

Q. What did Christ promise his disciples?

A. *John 14:18.* I will not leave you orphaned; I am coming to you.

Q. Was this promise only to the disciples or is it a common privilege of all believers?

A. *Isa. 57:15.* For thus says the high and lofty one who inhabits eternity, whose name is Holy: I dwell in the high and holy place, and also with those who are contrite and humble in spirit, to revive the spirit of the humble, and to revive the heart of the contrite.

2 Cor. 6:16b. For we are the temple of the living God; as God said, I will live in them and walk among them.

Rev. 3:20. Listen! I am standing at the door, knocking; if you hear my voice and open the door, I will come in to you and eat with you, and you with me.

Q. Does the apostle Paul speak of the Son of God being revealed in him?

A. *Gal. 1:15-16.* ...God, who had set me apart before I was born and called me through his grace, was pleased to reveal his Son in me,[28] so that I might proclaim him among the Gentiles.

---

[28] "*in me*" is an alternate reading in the NRSV. This seems closer to the Greek, and is the textual choice in NJerB. REB has "in and through me."

Q. Is it necessary to know Christ inwardly?

A. *2 Cor. 13:5.* Examine yourselves to see whether you are living in the faith. Test yourselves. Do you not realize that Jesus Christ is in you?—unless, indeed, you fail to meet the test!

Q. Did the apostle long for this inward birth to be experienced by others?

A. *Gal. 4:19.* My little children, for whom I am again in the pain of childbirth until Christ is formed in you,

Q. What does Paul say about needing an inward knowledge of Christ, and a new nature?

A. *2 Cor. 5:16-17.* From now on, therefore, we regard no one from a human point of view; even though we once knew Christ from a human point of view, we know him no longer in that way. So if anyone is in Christ, there is a new creation: everything old has passed away; see, everything has become new!

Eph. 4:20-24. That is not the way you learned Christ! For surely you have heard about him and were taught in him, as truth is in Jesus. You were taught to put away your former way of life, your old self, corrupt and deluded by its lusts, and to be renewed in the spirit of your minds, and to clothe yourselves with the new self, created according to the likeness of God in true righteousness and holiness.[29]

Q. Is Christ within that mystery of God and hope of glory the apostle preached?

A. *Col. 1:27-28a.* To them God chose to make known how great among the Gentiles are the riches of the glory of this mystery, which is Christ in you, the hope of glory. It is he whom we proclaim.[30]

---

[29] CEV: But that isn't what you were taught about Jesus Christ. He is truth, and you heard about him and learned about him. You were told that your foolish desires will destroy you and that you must give up your old way of life with all its bad habits. Let the Spirit change your way of thinking and make you into a new person. You were created to be like God, and so you must please him and be truly holy.

[30] REB: To them he chose to make known what a wealth of glory is offered to the Gentiles in this secret purpose: Christ in you, the hope of glory. He it is whom we proclaim.

Q. Does the apostle elsewhere emphasize the new birth?

A. *Rom. 13:14.* Instead, put on the Lord Jesus Christ, and make no provision for the flesh, to gratify its desires.[31]

Q. Did he write to any believers about having put off the old and put on the new person?

A. *Gal. 3:27.* As many of you as were baptized into Christ have clothed yourselves with Christ.

Col. 3:9-10. …you have stripped off the old self with its practices and have clothed yourselves with the new self, which is being renewed in knowledge according to the image of its creator.[32]

Q. Does Christ himself speak about the need for a new birth?

A. *John 3:3.* Jesus answered him, "Very truly, I tell you, no one can see the kingdom of God without being born from above."

Q. What seed does this birth come from?

A. *1 Pet. 1:23.* You have been born anew, not of perishable but of imperishable seed, through the living and enduring word of God.

Q. How does Paul testify about his own new life?

A. *Gal. 2:19b-20.* I have been crucified with Christ; and it is no longer I who live, but it is Christ who lives in me.[33]

Q. What does "preaching the cross of Christ" mean?

A. *1 Cor. 1:18.* For the message about the cross is foolishness to those who are perishing, but to us who are being saved it is the power of God.

---

[31] CEV: Let the Lord Jesus Christ be as near to you as the clothes you wear. Then you won't try to satisfy your selfish desires.

[32] REB: …you have discarded the old human nature and the conduct that goes with it, and have put on the new nature which is constantly being renewed in the image of its Creator and brought to know God.

[33] NJerB: I have been crucified with Christ and yet I am alive; yet it is no longer I, but Christ living in me.

Q. How did such preaching affect Paul? And how preferable is this to outward rituals?

A. *Gal. 6:14-15.* May I never boast of anything except the cross of our Lord Jesus Christ, by which the world has been crucified to me, and I to the world. For neither circumcision nor uncircumcision is anything; but a new creation is everything!

Q. What does Christ say about the unity of believers with him?

A. *John 14:20-23.* On that day you will know that I am in my Father, and you in me, and I in you.

John 15:4-5. Abide in me as I abide in you. Just as the branch cannot bear fruit by itself unless it abides in the vine, neither can you unless you abide in me. I am the vine, you are the branches. Those who abide in me and I in them bear much fruit, because apart from me you can do nothing.[34]

John 17:20-21. I ask not only on behalf of these, but also on behalf of those who will believe in me through their word, that they may all be one. As you, Father, are in me and I am in you, may they also be in us, so that the world may believe that you have sent me. The glory that you have given me I have given them, so that they may be one, as we are one, I in them and you in me, that they may become completely one, so that the world may know that you have sent me and have loved them even as you have loved me.[35]

Q. How does Paul describe this unity?

A. *Hebr. 2:11.* For the one who sanctifies and those who are sanctified all have one Father. For this reason Jesus is not ashamed to call them brothers and sisters....

---

[34] CEV: Stay joined to me, and I will stay joined to you. Just as a branch cannot produce fruit unless it stays joined to the vine, you cannot produce fruit unless you stay joined to me. I am the vine, and you are the branches. If you stay joined to me, and I stay joined to you, then you will produce lots of fruit. But you cannot do anything without me.

[35] CEV: I am not praying just for these followers, I am also praying for everyone else who will have faith because of what my followers will say about me. I want all of them to be one with each other, just as I am one with you and you are one with me. I also want them to be one with us. Then the people of this world will believe that you sent me.

Q. And what does Peter say?

A. *2 Pet. 1:4.* Thus he has given us, through these things, his precious and very great promises, so that through them you may escape from the corruption that is in the world because of lust, and may become participants of the divine nature.[36]

---

[36] CEV: God made great and marvelous promises, so that his nature would become part of us. Then we could escape our evil desires and the corrupt influences of this world.

Chapter Five

The Light by which Christ Enlightens Everyone: the Universality and Sufficiency of God's Grace

Q. What is the nature of God's love toward fallen and lost humanity?

A. *John 3:16.* For God so loved the world that he gave his only Son, so that everyone who believes in him may not perish but may have eternal life.

1 John 4:9. God's love was revealed among us in this way: God sent his only Son into the world so that we might live through him.

Q. Does the word "world" signify each and every person, or only a few?

A. *Hebr. 2:9.* ...we do see Jesus, who for a little while was made lower than the angels, now crowned with glory and honor because of the suffering of death, so that by the grace of God he might taste death for everyone.[37]

1 John 2:1-2. But if anyone does sin, we have an advocate with the Father, Jesus Christ the righteous; and he is the atoning sacrifice for our sins, and not for ours only but also for the sins of the whole world.

---

[37] NJerB: But we do see Jesus, who was for a short while made less than the angels, now crowned with glory and honor because he submitted to death, so that by God's grace his experience of death should benefit all humanity.

Q. Plainly John means by the world not only believers but everyone; what does Paul add?

A. *Col. 1:27, 28.* ...Christ in you, the hope of glory. It is he whom we proclaim, warning everyone and teaching everyone in all wisdom, so that we may present everyone mature in Christ.[38]

1 Tim. 2:1, 3, 4, 6. First of all, then, I urge that supplications, prayers, intercessions, and thanksgivings be made for everyone....This is right and is acceptable in the sight of God our Savior, who desires everyone to be saved and to come to the knowledge of the truth...who gave himself a ransom for all—this was attested at the right time.

Q. What is Peter's testimony?

A. *2 Pet. 3:9.* The Lord is not slow about his promise, as some think of slowness, but is patient with you, not wanting any to perish, but all to come to repentance.

Q. Are there more scriptures that attest to this?

A. *Ezek. 33:11.* Say to them, As I live, says the Lord God, I have no pleasure in the death of the wicked, but that the wicked turn from their ways and live.[39]

Ps. 145:8, 9. The Lord is gracious and merciful, slow to anger and abounding in steadfast love. The Lord is good to all, and his compassion is over all that he has made.

2 Cor. 5:19. ...in Christ God was reconciling the world to himself.[40]

---

[38] NAB: Christ in you, the hope of glory. It is he whom we proclaim, admonishing everyone and teaching everyone with all wisdom, that we may present everyone perfect in Christ.

[39] REB: Tell them: As I live, says the Lord God, I have no desire for the death of the wicked. I would rather that the wicked should mend their ways and live.

[40] CEV: God was in Christ, offering peace and forgiveness to the people of this world. And he has given us the work of sharing his message about peace.

Q. These scriptures seem to show that God's love extends to all, who might have been, or could be, saved by Christ. What then, is the scriptural response to those who claim that neither God's love nor Christ's sacrifice effect the justification of a large part of humanity, who are destined for condemnation, from cradle to grave?

A. *John 3:17.* Indeed, God did not send the Son into the world to condemn the world, but in order that the world might be saved through him.[41]

John 12:46, 47. I have come as light into the world, so that everyone who believes in me should not remain in the darkness. I do not judge anyone who hears my words and does not keep them, for I came not to judge the world, but to save the world.[42]

Q. What scriptures are used by those who contrive a position so contrary to truth?

A. *Rom. 9:11-13.* Even before they had been born or had done anything good or bad (so that God's purpose of election might continue, not by works but by his call) she was told, "The elder shall serve the younger." As it is written, "I have loved Jacob, but I have hated Esau."

Q. That passage merely stated that before the children were born it was decreed that the elder brother should serve the younger. The added words (Jacob have I loved, Esau have I hated) are from the prophet Malachi, who wrote hundreds of years after both brothers were dead. Doesn't scripture mention any other reason for hating Esau beyond God's own decree? What does this same apostle state elsewhere?

A. *Hebr. 12:16-17.* See to it that no one becomes like Esau, an immoral and Godless person, who sold his birthright for a single meal. You know that later, when he wanted to inherit the blessing, he was rejected.[43]

---

[41] NIV: For God did not send his Son into the world to condemn the world, but to save the world through him.

[42] CEV: I am the light that has come into the world. No one who has faith in me will stay in the dark. I am not the one who will judge those who refuse to obey my teachings. I came to save the people of this world, not to be their judge.

[43] NJerB: And be careful that there is no immoral person, or anyone worldly minded like Esau, who sold his birthright for one single meal. As you know, when he wanted to obtain the blessing afterwards, he was rejected.

Q. Others allege that because of Adam's sin many—even children—are condemned. Do not the scriptures declare that the death of Christ was as redemptive as Adam's sin was condemnatory?

A. *Rom. 5:15, 18.* For if the many died through the one man's trespass, much more surely have the grace of God and the free gift in the grace of the one man, Jesus Christ, abounded for the many. Therefore just as one man's trespass led to condemnation for all, so one man's act of righteousness leads to justification and life for all.[44]

Q. That passage alone would seem to offer abundant proof that Christ's death is sufficient to counter any harm brought upon humankind by Adam's sin. What then is cause for condemnation?

A. *John 3:18.* Those who believe in him are not condemned; but those who do not believe are condemned already, because they have not believed in the name of the only Son of God.

2 Thess. 2:10-12. ...and every kind of wicked deception for those who are perishing, because they refused to love the truth and so be saved. For this reason God sends them a powerful delusion, leading them to believe what is false, so that all who have not believed the truth but took pleasure in unrighteousness will be condemned.

Q. According to the scriptures, God's purpose in having his son Jesus Christ appear is to bring love and mercy to all, enabling them to receive this grace and be saved by it.

A. *Col. 1:23.* ...provided that you continue securely established and steadfast in the faith, without shifting from the hope promised by the gospel that you heard, which has been proclaimed to every creature under heaven. I, Paul, became a servant of this gospel.[45]

---

[44] For Rom. 5:18, REB: It follows, then, that as the result of one misdeed was condemnation for all people, so the result of one righteous act is acquittal and life for all.

[45] Living Bible: the only condition is that you fully believe the Truth, standing in it steadfast and firm, strong in the Lord, convinced of the Good News that Jesus died for you, and never shifting from trusting him to save you. This is the wonderful news that came to each of you and is now spreading all over the world. And I, Paul, have the joy of telling it to others.

Q. What is this gospel Paul talks about?

A. *Rom. 1:16.* For I am not ashamed of the gospel; it is the power of God for salvation to everyone who has faith.

Q. Is this gospel hidden?

A. *2 Cor. 4:3-4.* And even if our gospel is veiled, it is veiled to those who are perishing. In their case the God of this world has blinded the minds of the unbelievers, to keep them from seeing the light of the gospel of the glory of Christ.[46]

Q. Hasn't this Light come into the world? And aren't people condemned because they do not love it, not because it is hidden from them?

A. *John 3:19a.* And this is the judgment, that the light has come into the world and people loved darkness rather than light....

Q. Why don't they love it?

A. *John 3:19b.* ...because their deeds were evil.

Q. Is everyone enlightened by this Light?

A. *John 1:8-9.* He [John the Baptist] himself was not the light, but he came to testify to the light. The true light, which enlightens everyone, was coming into the world.

Q. Does this Light discover all things?

A. *Eph. 5:13-14a.* Everything exposed by the light becomes visible, for everything that becomes visible is light.[47]

---

[46] REB: If our gospel is veiled at all, it is veiled only for those on their way to destruction; their unbelieving minds are so blinded by the god of this passing age that the gospel of the glory of Christ, who is the image of God, cannot dawn upon them and bring them light.

[47] TEV: And when all things are brought out to the light, their true nature is clearly revealed; for anything that is clearly revealed becomes light.

Q. Do evil persons preach about this Light? Or heed it?

A. *John 3:20.* For all who do evil hate the light and do not come to the light, so that their deeds may not be exposed.

Job 24:13. There are those who rebel against the light.

Q. Do good people love and follow the Light?

A. *John 3:21.* But those who do what is true come to the light, so that it may be clearly seen that their deeds have been done in God.[48]

Q. What benefit comes to those who love and walk in the Light?

A. *1 John 1:7.* If we walk in the light as he himself is in the light, we have fellowship with one another, and the blood of Jesus his Son cleanses us from all sin.

Q. Does Christ command us to heed the Light?

A. *John 12:36a.* "While you have the light, believe in the light, so that you may become children of light."

Q. Were the apostles commanded to turn people to the Light?

A. *Acts 26:17-18.* I will rescue you from your people and from the Gentiles—to whom I am sending you to open their eyes so that they may turn from darkness to light and from the power of Satan to God, so that they may receive forgiveness of sins and a place among those who are sanctified by faith in me.[49]

Q. Does this Light remain with everyone throughout life, in order to save? Or only during their day of visitation?

---

[48] CEV: But everyone who lives by the truth will come to the light, because they want others to know that God is really the one doing what they do.

[49] CEV: The Lord also said, "I will protect you from the Jews and from the Gentiles that I am sending you to. I want you to open their eyes, so that they will turn from darkness to light and from the power of Satan to God. Then their sins will be forgiven, and by faith in me they will become part of God's holy people."

A. *John 12:35.* Jesus said to them, "The light is with you for a little longer. Walk while you have the light, so that the darkness may not overtake you."

Hebr. 4:7. Again he sets a certain day—"today"—saying through David much later, in the words already quoted, "Today, if you hear his voice, do not harden your hearts."

Q. How can it be established that there is a day when people may know things about their peace which later may be hidden from them?

A. *Luke 19:41-42.* As he came near and saw the city, he wept over it, saying, "If you, even you, had only recognized on this day the things that make for peace! But now they are hidden from your eyes."

Q. Is there any other scripture evidence for the Lord's willingness to gather a people who chose not to be gathered and therefore were condemned?

A. *Matt. 23:37 and Luke 13:34.* Jerusalem, Jerusalem, the city that kills the prophets and stones those who are sent to it! How often have I desired to gather your children together as a hen gathers her brood under her wings, and you were not willing!

Matt. 18:32-34. Then his Lord summoned him and said to him, "You wicked slave! I forgave you all that debt because you pleaded with me. Should you not have had mercy on your fellow slave, as I had mercy on you?" And in anger his Lord handed him over to be tortured until he would pay his entire debt.

Acts 13:46. Then both Paul and Barnabas spoke out boldly, saying, "It was necessary that the word of God should be spoken first to you. Since you reject it and judge yourselves to be unworthy of eternal life, we are now turning to the Gentiles."

Prov. 1:24-26. Because I have called and you refused, have stretched out my hand and no one heeded, and because you have ignored all my counsel and would have none of my reproof, I also will laugh at your calamity; I will mock when panic strikes you....[50]

---

[50] NJerB: Since I have called and you refused me, since I have beckoned and no one has taken notice, since you have ignored all my advice and rejected all my warnings, I, for my part, shall laugh at your distress, and I shall jeer when terror befalls you.

Jer. 18:9-10. And at another moment I may declare concerning a nation or a kingdom that I will build and plant it, but if it does evil in my sight, not listening to my voice, then I will change my mind about the good that I had intended to do to it.[51]

Q. Does God's Spirit strive with people for a time, and then forbear?

A. *Gen. 6:3.* Then the Lord said, "My spirit shall not abide in mortals forever."

Q. May God's Spirit be resisted?

A. *Acts 7:51* [Stephen speaking] "You stiff-necked people, uncircumcised in heart and ears, you are forever opposing the Holy Spirit, just as your ancestors used to do."

Rom. 1:18. For the wrath of God is revealed from heaven against all ungodliness and wickedness of those who by their wickedness suppress the truth.

Q. Has God shown people what can be known of him?

A. *Rom. 1:19.* For what can be known about God is plain to them, because God has shown it to them.

Q. Is this Light or seed sown in the hearts of evil persons?

A. *Matt. 13:3, 4, 5, 7.* And he told them many things in parables, saying: "Listen! A sower went out to sow. And as he sowed, some seeds fell on the path, and the birds came and ate them up. Other seeds fell on rocky ground, where they did not have much soil, and they sprang up quickly, since they had no depth of soil. Other seeds fell among thorns, and the thorns grew up and choked them."[52]

---

[51] CEV: If I promise to make a nation strong, but its people start disobeying me and doing evil, then I will change my mind and not help them at all.

[52] CEV: Then he told them many things by using stories. He said: "A farmer went out to scatter seed in a field. While the farmer was scattering the seed, some of it fell along the road and was eaten by birds. Other seeds fell on thin, rocky ground and quickly started growing because the soil wasn't very deep....Some other seeds fell where thorn bushes grew up and choked the plants."

Q. Are these places where the seed is said to have fallen to be understood as referring to the hearts of people?

A. *Matt. 13:18-19.* Hear then the parable of the sower. When anyone hears the word of the kingdom and does not understand it, the evil one comes and snatches away what is sown in the heart; this is what was sown on the path.

Q. Is this seed small when it first appears?

A. *Matt. 13:31.* ...The kingdom of heaven is like a mustard seed that someone took and sowed in his field; it is the smallest of all the seeds.

Q. Many do not understand what is meant by Light and seed. Although such metaphors are used frequently in the scriptures, they are not part of everyday speech. However, the question is whether a saving manifestation of the Spirit is given to all persons for their benefit?

A. *1 Cor. 12:7.* To each is given the manifestation of the Spirit for the common good.

Q. Certainly, if this Light and seed is for the good of everyone, it must be given in order to save. If it is not, or is insufficient to save, of what value is it? In this regard some Christians differentiate between a grace that is common, and a grace that is saving. Is there a grace which is both common to all people and brings salvation?

A. *Titus 2:11.* For the grace of God has appeared, bringing salvation to all.

Q. Anything which brings salvation must necessarily be saving. What are we taught by this grace?

A. *Titus 2:12.* ...training us to renounce impiety and worldly passions, and in the present age to live lives that are self-controlled, upright, and Godly.

Q. Certainly anything which teaches both righteousness and Godliness must be sufficient. For in these consist the whole duty of mankind. What does the apostle say elsewhere about this instruction?

A. *Acts 20:32.* And now I commend you to God and to the message of his grace, a message that is able to build you up and to give you the inheritance among all who are sanctified.

Q. What is the word of God?

A. *Hebr. 4:12-13.* Indeed, the word of God is living and active, sharper than any two-edged sword, piercing until it divides soul from spirit, joints from marrow; it is able to judge the thoughts and intentions of the heart. And before him no creature is hidden, but all are naked and laid bare to the eyes of the one to whom we must render an account.

Q. Shouldn't we heed God's word?

A. *2 Pet. 1:19.* So we have the prophetic message more fully confirmed. You will do well to be attentive to this as to a lamp shining in a dark place, until the day dawns and the morning star rises in your hearts.

Q. These scriptures seem very clear, both concerning the universality and the sufficiency of this Light, seed, grace, and word of God. But, is this saving word nearby or far away? Is it inward or outward?

A. *Rom. 10:6-8.* But the righteousness that comes from faith says, "Do not say in your heart, 'Who will ascend into heaven?'" (that is, to bring Christ down) "or 'Who will descend into the abyss?'" (that is, to bring Christ up from the dead). But what does it say? "The word is near you, on your lips and in your heart" that is, the word of faith that we proclaim.

Q. That passage is certainly clear about such a word. Does any scripture speak of the Light as being inward?

A. *2 Cor. 4:6-7.* For it is the God who said, "Let light shine out of darkness," who has shone in our hearts to give the light of the knowledge of the glory of God in the face of Jesus Christ. But we have this treasure in clay jars, so that it may be made clear that this extraordinary power belongs to God and does not come from us.

Q. Because it is also called the seed of the Kingdom, is the Kingdom of God also within?

A. *Luke 17:20b-21.* [Jesus said] "The kingdom of God is not coming with things that can be observed; nor will they say, 'Look, here it is!' or 'There it is!' For, in fact, the kingdom of God is within you."[53]

---

[53] In the NRSV this is the alternate reading to "the kingdom of God is among you." It is comparable to the rendering of the King James Version, which Barclay used.

Chapter Six

Faith, Justification, and Works

Q. What is faith?

A. *Hebr. 11:1.* Now faith is the assurance of things hoped for, the conviction of things not seen.

Q. Is faith absolutely necessary?

A. *Hebr. 11:6.* And without faith it is impossible to please God, for whoever would approach him must believe that he exists and that he rewards those who seek him.

Q. Are we justified by faith?

A. *Gal. 3:24.* Therefore the law was our disciplinarian until Christ came, so that we might be justified by faith.[54]

Q. What kind of faith counts for justification?

A. *Gal. 5:6.* For in Christ Jesus neither circumcision nor uncircumcision counts for anything; the only thing that counts is faith working through love.

Q. Are works as well as faith necessary for justification?

A. *James 2:20-24.* Do you want to be shown, you senseless person, that faith apart from works is barren? Was not our ancestor Abraham justified by works when he offered his son Isaac on the altar? You see that faith was active along with his works, and faith was brought to completion by the works. Thus the scripture was fulfilled that says, "Abraham

---

[54] Phillips: The Law was a strict tutor in charge of us until we went to the school of Christ and learned to be justified by faith in him.

believed God, and it was reckoned to him as righteousness," and he was called the friend of God. You see that a person is justified by works and not by faith alone.[55]

Q. Faith and works being equally required for justification, what kind of works does the apostle exclude?

A. *Rom. 3:20a.* For "no human being will be justified in his sight" by deeds prescribed by the law....

Q. Isn't it to exclude boasting that deeds of the law do not justify, and in order that God's grace may be exalted?

A. *Eph. 2:8-10.* For by grace you have been saved through faith, and this is not your own doing; it is the gift of God—not the result of works, so that no one may boast. For we are what he has made us, created in Christ Jesus for good works, which God prepared beforehand to be our way of life.[56]

Q. Are even the works performed by grace excluded? Are we never said to be saved or justified by them?

A. *Titus 3:5-7.* He saved us, not because of any works of righteousness that we had done, but according to his mercy, through the water of rebirth and renewal by the Holy Spirit. This Spirit he poured out on us richly through Jesus Christ our Savior, so that, having been justified by his grace, we might become heirs according to the hope of eternal life.

---

[55] CEV: Does some stupid person want proof that faith without deeds is useless? Well, our ancestor Abraham pleased God by putting his son Isaac on the altar to sacrifice him. Now you see how Abraham's faith and deeds worked together. He proved that his faith was real by what he did. This is what the Scriptures mean by saying, "Abraham had faith in God, and God was pleased with him." That's how Abraham became God's friend. You can now see that we please God by what we do and not only by what we believe.

[56] TEV: For it is by God's grace that you have been saved, through faith. It is not your own doing, but God's gift. There is nothing here to boast of, since it is not the result of your own efforts. God is our Maker, and in our union with Christ Jesus he has created us for a life of good works, which he has already prepared for us to do.

Q. To be justified by grace means to be saved, regenerated, which cannot exclude works done by grace and by the Spirit. In the following verses, how does the apostle maintain this balance against those who quibble about the law?

A. *Titus 3:8-9.* The saying is sure. I desire that you insist on these things, so that those who have come to believe in God may be careful to devote themselves to good works; these things are excellent and profitable to everyone. But avoid stupid controversies, genealogies, dissension, and quarrels about the law, for they are unprofitable and worthless.

Q. Does the apostle Paul, who is so much against justification by works of the law, say anything anywhere else about being justified by the Spirit?

A. *1 Cor. 6:11.* ...But you were washed, you were sanctified, you were justified in the name of the Lord Jesus Christ and in the Spirit of our God.

Q. Since the law gives neither the power nor the ability to obey, and thus falls short of justification; is there any power under the gospel by which the righteousness of the law comes to be fulfilled inwardly?

A. *Rom. 8:3-4.* For God has done what the law, weakened by the flesh, could not do: by sending his own Son in the likeness of sinful flesh, and to deal with sin, he condemned sin in the flesh, so that the just requirement of the law might be fulfilled in us, who walk not according to the flesh but according to the Spirit.

Q. Are not Spirit-empowered works a condition of life in the new covenant?

A. *Rom. 8:13.* for if you live according to the flesh, you will die; but if by the Spirit you put to death the deeds of the body, you will live.

Q. Does not the apostle frequently propose life to people on condition of repentance and other works?

A. *Acts 3:19.* Repent therefore, and turn to God so that your sins may be wiped out,

Rom. 8:17. ...and if children, then heirs, heirs of God and joint heirs with Christ—if, in fact, we suffer with him so that we may also be glorified with him.

2 Tim. 2:11, 12, 21. The saying is sure: If we have died with him, we will also live with him; if we endure, we will also reign with him; if we deny him, he will also deny us....All who cleanse themselves of the things I have mentioned will become special utensils, dedicated and useful to the owner of the house, ready for every good work.

Rev. 2:5. Remember then from what you have fallen; repent, and do the works you did at first. If not, I will come to you and remove your lampstand from its place, unless you repent.

Q. From these passages it appears the apostle excludes from justification only legalistic righteousness, not good deeds directed by Christ within us. Although not absolutely meritorious, are not these works the fruit of grace and judged of God to be worthy of reward?

A. *Ezek. 18:5-9.* If a man is righteous and does what is lawful and right—if he does not eat upon the mountains or lift up his eyes to the idols of the house of Israel, does not defile his neighbor's wife or approach a woman during her menstrual period, does not oppress anyone, but restores to the debtor his pledge, commits no robbery, gives his bread to the hungry and covers the naked with a garment, does not take advance or accrued interest, withholds his hand from iniquity, executes true justice between contending parties, follows my statutes, and is careful to observe my ordinances, acting faithfully—such a one is righteous; he shall surely live, says the Lord God.

Matt. 16:27. For the Son of Man is to come with his angels in the glory of his Father, and then he will repay everyone for what has been done.

Acts 10:34-35. Then Peter began to speak to them: "I truly understand that God shows no partiality but in every nation anyone who fears him and does what is right is acceptable to him."

Rom. 2:5b, 6, 7, 10. God's righteous judgment will be revealed. For he will repay according to each one's deeds: to those who by patiently doing good seek for glory and honor and immortality, he will give eternal life ...but glory and honor and peace for everyone who does good, the Jew first and also the Greek.

2 Cor. 5:10. For all of us must appear before the judgment seat of Christ, so that each may receive recompense for what has been done in the body, whether good or evil.

2 Thess. 1:5. This is evidence of the righteous judgment of God, and is intended to make you worthy of the kingdom of God, for which you are also suffering.[57]

James 1:25. But those who look into the perfect law, the law of liberty, and persevere, being not hearers who forget but doers who act—they will be blessed in their doing.

Hebr. 10:35. Do not, therefore, abandon that confidence of yours: it brings a great reward.

1 Pet. 1:17. If you invoke as Father the one who judges all people impartially according to their deeds, live in reverent fear during the time of your exile.[58]

Rev. 22:12, 14. See, I am coming soon; my reward is with me, to repay according to everyone's work. Blessed are those who wash their robes, so that they will have the right to the tree of life and may enter the city by the gates.

Q. It would seem to be God's purpose in sending the Son, the Lord Jesus Christ, not simply to save people by a wholly external imputed righteousness but also by an inward imparted righteousness, by the washing of regeneration. What more do the scriptures say about this?

A. *Matt. 1:21.* She [Mary] will bear a son, and you are to name him Jesus, for he will save his people from their sins.

Titus 2:13-14. We wait for the blessed hope and the manifestation of the glory of our great God and Savior, Jesus Christ. He it is who gave himself for us that he might redeem us from all iniquity and purify for himself a people of his own who are zealous for good deeds.

---

[57] NJerB: It all shows that God's judgment is just, so that you may be found worthy of the kingdom of God; it is for the sake of this that you are suffering now.

[58] REB: If you say "Father" to him who judges everyone impartially on the basis of what they have done, you must live in awe of him during your time on earth.

Chapter Seven

Perfection, or Freedom from Sin

Q. Clearly, from all the previously mentioned scriptures Christ, in addition to purchasing pardon for our sins, has also obtained the power which cleanses us from their filth. May we then expect to be freed from the dominion of sin in this life?

A. *Rom. 6:14a.* For sin will have no dominion over you ...

Q. For what reason?

A. *Rom 6:14b.* ...since you are not under law but under grace.

Q. Why then does the apostle ask about and complain of sin, saying, "Who shall deliver me from the body of this death?" Does he refer to that as a permanent condition for him and other believers, or is he referring only to what he had experienced? What does he say later?

A. *Rom. 8:1-2.* There is therefore now no condemnation for those who are in Christ Jesus.

For the law of the Spirit of life in Christ Jesus has set you free from the law of sin and of death.

Rom. 8:35-39. Who will separate us from the love of Christ? Will hardship, or distress, or persecution, or famine, or nakedness, or peril, or sword? As it is written, "For your sake we are being killed all day long; we are accounted as sheep to be slaughtered." No, in all these things we are more than conquerors through him who loved us. For I am convinced that neither death, nor life, nor angels, nor rulers, nor things present, nor things to come, nor powers, nor height, nor depth, nor anything else in all creation, will be able to separate us from the love of God in Christ Jesus our Lord.

Q. What does the apostle say to those, who taking occasion from his words, plead for the continuation of sin for life, and who think that being under grace they will be saved by the righteousness of Christ imputed to them?

A. *Rom. 6:15.* What then? Should we sin because we are not under law but under grace? By no means!

Q. Far from supposing sin is to be his constant condition, or that of all the believers, doesn't the apostle even suppose that many who were then of the church of Rome, to whom he wrote, were free from sin? What does he say then in relation to this matter?

A. *Rom. 6:2–7, 11-13, 16-22.* How can we who died to sin go on living in it? Do you not know that all of us who have been baptized into Christ Jesus were baptized into his death? Therefore we have been buried with him by baptism into death, so that, just as Christ was raised from the dead by the glory of the Father, so we too might walk in newness of life. For if we have been united with him in a death like his, we will certainly be united with him in a resurrection like his. We know that our old self was crucified with him so that the body of sin might be destroyed, and we might no longer be enslaved to sin. For whoever has died is freed from sin….So you also must consider yourselves dead to sin and alive to God in Christ Jesus. Therefore, do not let sin exercise dominion in your mortal bodies, to make you obey their passions. No longer present your members to sin as instruments of wickedness, but present yourselves to God as those who have been brought from death to life, and present your members to God as instruments of righteousness.…Do you not know that if you present yourselves to anyone as obedient slaves, you are slaves of the one whom you obey, either of sin, which leads to death, or of obedience, which leads to righteousness? But thanks be to God that you, having once been slaves of sin, have become obedient from the heart to the form of teaching to which you were entrusted, and that you, having been set free from sin, have become slaves of righteousness. I am speaking in human terms because of your natural limitations. For just as you once presented your members as slaves to impurity and to greater and greater iniquity, so now present your members as slaves to righteousness for sanctification. When you were slaves of sin, you were free in regard to righteousness. So what advantage did you then get from the things of which you now are ashamed? The end of those things is death. But now that you have been freed from sin and enslaved to God, the advantage you get is sanctification. The end is eternal life. For the wages of sin is death, but the free gift of God is eternal life in Christ Jesus our Lord.

Q. It would appear then that God requires us to be perfect.

A. *Matt. 5:48.* Be perfect, therefore, as your heavenly Father is perfect.

Q. Is it possible then to keep the commandments?

A. *Matt. 11:30.* For my yoke is easy, and my burden is light.

1 John 5:3. For the love of God is this, that we obey his commandments. And his commandments are not burdensome.

Q. Is it necessary for salvation to keep the commandments?

A. *Rev. 22:14.* Blessed are those who wash their robes, so that they will have the right to the tree of life and may enter the city by the gates.[59]

Q. Is the meaning of perfection to have kept the commandments, so as never to have sinned?

A. *1 John 1:10.* If we say that we have not sinned, we make him a liar, and his word is not in us.

---

[59] The King James Version, which Barclay used, reads, "who keep his commandments." Because in the Greek this phrase is strikingly similar to "who wash their robes," Bible scholars believe a copying error occurred. Modern versions follow a more definitive text. This symbolic phrase also implies obedience in appropriating the grace God offers.

Q. Do you understand that those who are perfect may say that they have no sin? Or only that they once sinned, as the apostle mentions in the passage cited? Notwithstanding this, may they not only come to know forgiveness for the guilt, but also cleansing from its filth?

A. *1 John 1:8-9.* If we say that we have no sin, we deceive ourselves, and the truth is not in us. If we confess our sins, he who is faithful and just will forgive us our sins and cleanse us from all unrighteousness.

Q. This scripture seems to be very plain when it is compared with the other one previously mentioned. However because some are apt to mistake and twist these words of the apostle, what does he say elsewhere? Was it his judgment that anyone could know God, or be a true Christian, who did not keep the commandments?

A. *1 John 2:1, 3, 4, 6.* My little children, I am writing these things to you so that you may not sin. But if anyone does sin, we have an advocate with the Father, Jesus Christ the righteous. Now by this we may be sure that we know him, if we obey his commandments. Whoever says, "I have come to know him," but does not obey his commandments, is a liar, and in such a person the truth does not exist....whoever says, "I abide in him," ought to walk just as he walked.

1 John 3:2-10. Beloved, we are God's children now; what we will be has not yet been revealed. What we do know is this: when he is revealed, we will be like him, for we will see him as he is. And all who have this hope in him purify themselves, just as he is pure. Everyone who commits sin is guilty of lawlessness; sin is lawlessness. You know that he was revealed to take away sins, and in him there is no sin. No one who abides in him sins; no one who sins has either seen him or known him. Little children, let no one deceive you. Everyone who does what is right is righteous, just as he is righteous. Everyone who commits sin is a child of the devil; for the devil has been sinning from the beginning. The Son of God was revealed for this purpose, to destroy the works of the devil. Those who have been born of God do not sin, because God's seed abides in them; they cannot sin, because they have been born of God. The children of God and the children of the devil are revealed in this way: all who do not do what is right are not from God, nor are those who do not love their brothers and sisters.

Q. It is very clear from these passages, that the apostles were certainly of another mind than those who plead for sin throughout life. And they were much against the deceit of those who want to consider themselves good Christians and nevertheless continue to live in their sins.

A. *Matt. 7:21, 24.* Not everyone who says to me, "Lord, Lord," will enter the kingdom of heaven, but only the one who does the will of my Father in heaven. Everyone then who hears these words of mine and acts on them will be like a wise man who built his house on rock.

John 13:17. If you know these things, you are blessed if you do them.

Q. What else does the apostle Paul say about the need to do God's will?

A. *1 Cor. 7:19.* Circumcision is nothing, and uncircumcision is nothing; but obeying the commandments of God is everything.[60]

Q. According to the apostle Paul was it not the very intention of Christ to have his church and children pure and without spot?

A. *Eph. 1:4.* Just as he chose us in Christ before the foundation of the world to be holy and blameless before him in love.[61]

Eph. 5:25-27. Husbands, love your wives, just as Christ loved the church and gave himself up for her, in order to make her holy by cleansing her with the washing of water by the word, so as to present the church to himself in splendor, without a spot or wrinkle or anything of the kind—yes, so that she may be holy and without blemish.

Q. Doesn't Paul press this matter further in addition to the passages already cited?

A. *2 Cor. 7:1; 2 Cor. 13:11; Col. 1:27b-28; 4:12 [blended].* Since we have these promises, beloved, let us cleanse ourselves from every defilement of body and of spirit, making holiness perfect in the fear of God.... Finally, brothers and sisters, farewell. Put things in order, listen to my appeal, agree with one another, live in peace; and the God of love and peace will be with you....Christ in you the hope of glory; it is he whom

---

[60] This symbolic language refers to those within and outside the old covenant, Jew and Gentile.
[61] CEV. Before the world was created, God had Christ choose us to live with him and to be his holy and innocent and loving people.

we proclaim, warning everyone and teaching everyone in all wisdom, so that we may present everyone mature in Christ....[like] Epaphras,... always wrestling in his prayers on your behalf, so that you may stand mature and fully assured in everything that God wills.

1 Thess. 3:13; 5:23. And may he so strengthen your hearts in holiness that you may be blameless before our God and Father at the coming of our Lord Jesus with all his saints. May the God of peace himself sanctify you entirely; and may your spirit and soul and body be kept sound and blameless at the coming of our Lord Jesus Christ.[62]

Q. Isn't this the very purpose for which God appointed teachers in his church?

A. *Eph. 4:11-13.* The gifts he gave were that some would be apostles, some prophets, some evangelists, some pastors and teachers, to equip the saints for the work of ministry, for building up the body of Christ, until all of us come to the unity of the faith and of the knowledge of the Son of God, to maturity, to the measure of the full stature of Christ.

Q. Because this is stressed so much, isn't it the testimony of scripture—which cannot lie—that some of the believers were free from sin at times? They were not always sinning as some have supposed.

A. *Gen. 6:9.* These are the descendants of Noah. Noah was a righteous man, blameless in his generation; Noah walked with God.

Job 1:8. The Lord said to Satan, "Have you considered my servant Job? There is no one like him on the earth, a blameless and upright man who fears God and turns away from evil."

Luke 1:5-6. In the days of King Herod of Judea, there was a priest named Zechariah, who belonged to the priestly order of Abijah. His wife was a descendant of Aaron, and her name was Elizabeth. Both of them were righteous before God, living blamelessly according to all the commandments and regulations of the Lord.

---

[62] NIV: May he give you inner strength that you may be blameless and holy in the presence of our God and Father when our Lord Jesus comes with all his holy ones....May God himself, the God of peace, sanctify you through and through. May your whole spirit, soul and body be kept blameless at the coming of our Lord Jesus Christ.

Q. That should be sufficient evidence regarding a few persons in particular. But, does scripture suggest that this is possible even for many people?

A. *Eph. 2:4-6.* But God, who is rich in mercy, out of the great love with which he loved us even when we were dead through our trespasses, made us alive together with Christ—by grace you have been saved—and raised us up with him and seated us with him in the heavenly places in Christ Jesus.

Hebr. 12:22-23. But you have come to Mount Zion and to the city of the living God, the heavenly Jerusalem, and to innumerable angels in festal gathering, and to the assembly of the firstborn who are enrolled in heaven, and to God the judge of all, and to the spirits of the righteous made perfect.

Rev. 14:1, 4-5. Then I looked, and there was the Lamb, standing on Mount Zion! And with him were one hundred forty-four thousand who had his name and his Father's name written on their foreheads….It is these who have not defiled themselves with women, for they are virgins; these follow the Lamb wherever he goes. They have been redeemed from humankind as first fruits for God and the Lamb, and in their mouth no lie was found; they are blameless.

Chapter Eight

Perseverance and Falling from Grace

Q. Is it enough for believers to be sure that they once received true grace? Or is any further certainty required?

A. *2 Pet. 1:10.* Therefore, brothers and sisters, be all the more eager to confirm your call and election, for if you do this, you will never stumble.

Q. May those who have received true grace have reason to fear they could fall?

A. *1 Cor. 9:27.* But I punish my body and enslave it, so that after proclaiming to others I myself should not be disqualified.[63]

Q. That greatly contradicts the doctrine of those who say, "Once in grace, always in grace." But, does the apostle Paul express this simply out of personal humility? Or does he consider that this can be true for other Christians as well?

A. *Hebr. 3:12-13.* Take care, brothers and sisters, that none of you may have an evil, unbelieving heart that turns away from the living God. But exhort one another every day, as long as it is called "today," so that none of you may be hardened by the deceitfulness of sin.

Hebr. 4:11. Let us therefore make every effort to enter that rest, so that no one may fall through such disobedience as theirs.

Hebr. 6:4-6, 12-15. For it is impossible to restore again to repentance those who have once been enlightened, and have tasted the heavenly gift, and have shared in the Holy Spirit, and have tasted the goodness of the word of God and the powers of the age to come, and then have fallen away, since on their own they are crucifying again the Son of God and

---

[63] REB: I do not spare my body, but bring it under strict control, for fear that after preaching to others I should find myself disqualified.

are holding him up to contempt....so that you may not become sluggish, but imitators of those who through faith and patience inherit the promises.

Hebr. 12:15. See to it that no one fails to obtain the grace of God; that no root of bitterness springs up and causes trouble, and through it many become defiled.

Q. Is this just conjecture? Or, does the apostle affirm this to be not only possible but certain?

A. *2 Tim. 4:3-4.* For the time is coming when people will not put up with sound doctrine, but having itching ears, they will accumulate for themselves teachers to suit their own desires, and will turn away from listening to the truth and wander away to myths.

Q. Does the apostle consider it necessary to guard even someone like his beloved Timothy against this hazard?

A. *1 Tim. 1:18-19.* I am giving you these instructions, Timothy, my child, in accordance with the prophecies made earlier about you, so that by following them you may fight the good fight, having faith and a good conscience. By rejecting conscience, certain persons have suffered shipwreck in the faith;

1 Tim. 6:10. For the love of money is a root of all kinds of evil, and in their eagerness to be rich some have wandered away from the faith and pierced themselves with many pains.[64]

2 Tim. 2:17-18. ...and their talk will spread like gangrene. Among them are Hymenaeus and Philetus, who have swerved from the truth by claiming that the resurrection has already taken place. They are upsetting the faith of some.[65]

---

[64] REB: The love of money is the root of all evil, and in pursuit of it some have wandered from the faith and spiked themselves on many a painful thorn.

[65] CEV: That sort of talk is like a sore that won't heal. And Hymenaeus and Philetus have been talking this way by teaching that the dead have already been raised to life. This is far from the truth, and it is destroying the faith of some people.

Q. Is there anywhere that the apostle expresses a fear that this might happen to any number of people who once truly received the faith of Christ?

A. *Rom. 11:20.* That is true. They were broken off because of their unbelief, but you stand only through faith. So do not become proud, but stand in awe.

1 Tim. 4:1. Now the Spirit expressly says that in later times some will renounce the faith by paying attention to deceitful spirits and teachings of demons,

1 Thess. 3:5. For this reason, when I could bear it no longer, I sent to find out about your faith; I was afraid that somehow the tempter had tempted you and that our labor had been in vain.

Q. Does the apostle Peter think that some who have known the right way may forsake it?

A. *2 Pet. 2:14b-15, 17-22.* Accursed children! They have left the straight road and have gone astray, following the road of Balaam son of Bosor, who loved the wages of doing wrong....These are waterless springs and mists driven by a storm; for them the deepest darkness has been reserved. For they speak bombastic nonsense, and with licentious desires of the flesh they entice people who have just escaped from those who live in error. They promise them freedom, but they themselves are slaves of corruption; for people are slaves to whatever masters them. For if, after they have escaped the defilements of the world through the knowledge of our Lord and Savior Jesus Christ, they are again entangled in them and overpowered, the last state has become worse for them than the first. For it would have been better for them never to have known the way of righteousness than, after knowing it, to turn back from the holy commandment that was passed on to them. It has happened to them according to the true proverb, "The dog turns back to its own vomit," and, "The sow is washed only to wallow in the mud."

Q. Does Peter caution those who are steadfast that even they might fall?

A. *2 Pet. 3:17.* You therefore, beloved, since you are forewarned, beware that you are not carried away with the error of the lawless and lose your own stability.

Q. May a person be truly a branch in Christ—or a real member of his body—and later be cut off?

A. *John 15:6.* Whoever does not abide in me is thrown away like a branch and withers.⁶⁶

Q. May a righteous person depart from righteousness?

A. *Ezek. 18:26.* When the righteous turn away from their righteousness and commit iniquity, they shall die for it; for the iniquity that they have committed they shall die.

Ezek. 33:13. Though I say to the righteous that they shall surely live, yet if they trust in their righteousness and commit iniquity, none of their righteous deeds shall be remembered; but in the iniquity that they have committed they shall die.

Q. May a believer come to a condition in this life from which it is impossible to fall away?

A. *Rev. 3:12.* If you conquer, I will make you a pillar in the temple of my God; you will never go out of it. I will write on you the name of my God, and the name of the city of my God, the new Jerusalem that comes down from my God out of heaven, and my own new name.

Q. Is it possible for persons to be assured that they are in this condition?

A. *Rom. 8:38-39.* For I am convinced that neither death, nor life, nor angels, nor rulers, nor things present, nor things to come, nor powers, nor height, nor depth, nor anything else in all creation, will be able to separate us from the love of God in Christ Jesus our Lord.

---

⁶⁶ NJerB: Anyone who does not remain in me is thrown away like a branch—and withers.

Chapter Nine

The Church and Ministry

Q. What is the church?

A. *1 Tim. 3:14b-15.* I am writing these instructions to you so that, if I am delayed, you may know how one ought to behave in the household of God, which is the church of the living God, the pillar and bulwark of the truth.

Q. Who is the head of the church?

A. *Col. 1:13, 18; 2:19.* He has rescued us from the power of darkness and transferred us into the kingdom of his beloved Son ...He is the head of the body, the church...from whom the whole body, nourished and held together by its ligaments and sinews, grows with a growth that is from God.

Q. What kind of persons make up the church?

A. *1 Cor. 1:2.* Those who are sanctified in Christ Jesus.

Acts 2:47. And day by day the Lord added to their number those who were being saved.

Q. Has Christ appointed officers in the church for the work of ministry?

A. *Eph. 4:8, 11-12.* Therefore it is said, "When he ascended on high he made captivity itself a captive; he gave gifts to his people." ...The gifts he gave were that some would be apostles, some prophets, some evangelists, some pastors and teachers, to equip the saints for the work of ministry, for building up the body of Christ.

Q. What kind of people should the teachers and overseers of the church be?

A. *1 Tim. 3:2-7.* Now a bishop must be above reproach, married only once, temperate, sensible, respectable, hospitable, an apt teacher, not a drunkard, not violent but gentle, not quarrelsome, and not a lover of money. He must manage his own household well, keeping his children submissive and respectful in every way—for if someone does not know how to manage his own household, how can he take care of God's church? He must not be a recent convert, or he may be puffed up with conceit and fall into the condemnation of the devil. Moreover, he must be well thought of by outsiders, so that he may not fall into disgrace and the snare of the devil.

Titus 1:7-9. For a bishop, as God's steward, must be blameless; he must not be arrogant or quick-tempered or addicted to wine or violent or greedy for gain; but he must be hospitable, a lover of goodness, prudent, upright, devout, and self-controlled. He must have a firm grasp of the word that is trustworthy in accordance with the teaching, so that he may be able both to preach with sound doctrine and to refute those who contradict it.

Q. What is obligatory upon such persons?

A. *Acts 20:28.* Keep watch over yourselves and over all the flock, of which the Holy Spirit has made you overseers, to shepherd the church of God.

1 Pet. 5:1-3. Now as an elder myself and a witness of the sufferings of Christ, as well as one who shares in the glory to be revealed, I exhort the elders among you to tend the flock of God that is in your charge, exercising the oversight, not under compulsion but willingly, as God would have you do it—not for sordid gain but eagerly. Do not lord it over those in your charge but be examples to the flock.

Q. Although they are not to lord it over the flock, nevertheless isn't respect due them because of their leadership role?

A. *1 Tim. 5:17.* Let the elders who rule well be considered worthy of double honor, especially those who labor in preaching and teaching.

Q. Even though among true Christians everyone who believes should have the witness in themselves and be advised in themselves by the Spirit, shouldn't there also be real submission of one to another in the Lord?

A. *1 Cor. 14:32.* And the spirits of prophets are subject to the prophets....

Hebr. 13:17. Obey your leaders and submit to them, for they are keeping watch over your souls and will give an account. Let them do this with joy and not with sighing—for that would be harmful to you.

1 Thess. 5:12-13a. But we appeal to you, brothers and sisters, to respect those who labor among you, and have charge of you in the Lord and admonish you; esteem them very highly in love because of their work....

1 Pet. 5:5. In the same way, you who are younger must accept the authority of the elders. And all of you must clothe yourselves with humility in your dealings with one another, for God opposes the proud, but gives grace to the humble.

Q. How should true teachers minister in the church?

A. *1 Pet. 4:10-11.* Like good stewards of the manifold grace of God, serve one another with whatever gift each of you has received. Whoever speaks must do so as one speaking the very words of God; whoever serves must do so with the strength that God supplies, so that God may be glorified in all things through Jesus Christ.[67]

Q. It would seem that all true ministers of the church of Christ should minister from the gift and grace of God which they have received. Some consider natural wisdom or talents and human learning to be qualifications absolutely necessary for a minister. But they do not consider grace to be absolutely necessary and think that one may be a minister without it. What does scripture say about that?

A. *Titus 1:7-8b.* For a bishop, as God's steward, must be blameless...[sober] ...upright, devout...and self-controlled.

---

[67] CEV: Each of you has been blessed with one of God's many wonderful gifts to be used in the service of others. So use your gift well. If you have the gift of speaking, preach God's message. If you have the gift of helping others, do it with the strength that God supplies. Everything should be done in a way that will bring honor to God because of Jesus Christ, who is glorious and powerful forever. Amen.

Q. It would seem impossible for someone to be just, holy, serious-minded, and temperate without the grace of God. If these qualifications are absolutely necessary, surely a person cannot be qualified without having them. What does scripture say about the need for natural wisdom and human learning?

A. *1 Cor. 1:20-21.* Where is the one who is wise? Where is the scribe? Where is the debater of this age? Has not God made foolish the wisdom of the world? For since, in the wisdom of God, the world did not know God through wisdom, God decided, through the foolishness of our proclamation, to save those who believe.[68]

Q. It seems therefore that ministers are not enabled to preach well just by wisdom and learning, even though great skill in learning has been deemed vital for crafting a good sermon. What is the apostle's judgment on this?

A. *1 Cor. 1:17.* For Christ did not send me to baptize but to proclaim the gospel, and not with eloquent wisdom, so that the cross of Christ might not be emptied of its power.

1 Cor. 2:3-5. And I came to you in weakness and in fear and in much trembling. My speech and my proclamation were not with plausible words of wisdom, but with a demonstration of the Spirit and of power, so that your faith might rest not on human wisdom but on the power of God.[69]

Q. The apostle puts more stress upon the demonstration and power of the Spirit in a preacher than upon training in human literature. Does that mean that ministers should preach as the Spirit teaches?

A. *1 Cor. 2:13.* And we speak of these things in words not taught by human wisdom but taught by the Spirit.

---

[68] NJerB: Where are the philosophers? Where are the experts? And where are the debaters of this age? Do you not see how God has shown up human wisdom as folly? Since in the wisdom of God the world was unable to recognize God through wisdom, it was God's own pleasure to save believers thrugh the folly of the Gospel.

[69] NJerB: I came among you in weakness, fear, and in great trembling and what I spoke and proclaimed was not meant to convince by philosophical argument but to demonstrate the convincing power of the Spirit, so that your faith should depend not on human wisdom but on the power of God.

Acts 2:4. All of them were filled with the Holy Spirit and began to speak in other languages, as the Spirit gave them ability.

Q. Is it Christ who speaks in and through his ministers?

A. *Matt. 10:20.* ...for it is not you who speak, but the Spirit of your Father speaking through you.[70]

Mark 13:11b. ...For it is not you who speak, but the Holy Spirit.

Luke 12:12. For the Holy Spirit will teach you at that very hour what you ought to say.

2 Cor. 13:3. ...you desire proof that Christ is speaking in me. He is not weak in dealing with you, but is powerful in you.

Q. So said Paul. What is his opinion of the human learning which some praise so highly and consider essential for a minister?

A. *Col. 2:8.* See to it that no one takes you captive through philosophy and empty deceit, according to human tradition, according to the elemental spirits of the universe, and not according to Christ.[71]

1 Tim. 6:20. Timothy, guard what has been entrusted to you. Avoid the profane chatter and contradictions of what is falsely called knowledge;

Q. Although true ministers do not speak by the natural human wisdom, does this mean their testimony is wholly void of wisdom?

A. *1 Cor. 2:6-7.* Yet among the mature we do speak wisdom, though it is not a wisdom of this age or of the rulers of this age, who are doomed to perish. But we speak God's wisdom, secret and hidden, which God decreed before the ages for our glory.[72]

---

[70] CEV: But you will not really be the one speaking. The Spirit from your Father will tell you what to say.

[71] NIV: See to it that no one takes you captive through hollow and deceptive philosophy, which depends on human tradition and the basic principles of the world rather than on Christ.

[72] CEV: We do use wisdom when speaking to people who are mature in their faith. But it isn't the wisdom of this world or of its rulers, who will soon disappear. We speak of God's hidden and mysterious wisdom that God decided to use for our glory long before the world began.

Q. Why is a person incapable of ministering the things of God solely by natural wisdom?

A. *1 Cor. 2:11, 14.* For what human being knows what is truly human except the human spirit that is within? So also no one comprehends what is truly God's except the Spirit of God....Those who are unspiritual do not receive the gifts of God's Spirit, for they are foolishness to them, and they are unable to understand them because they are spiritually discerned.

Q. These scriptures maintain sufficiently that the true call to the ministry is from God. That a true minister is made by the gift and grace of God. That true and effective preaching comes from the inward teaching and leading of the Spirit of God. But, what does scripture say about the maintenance of ministers?

A. *Gal. 6:6.* Those who are taught the word must share in all good things with their teacher.

1 Cor. 9:11-14. If we have sown spiritual good among you, is it too much if we reap your material benefits? If others share this rightful claim on you, do not we still more? Nevertheless, we have not made use of this right, but we endure anything rather than put an obstacle in the way of the gospel of Christ. Do you not know that those who are employed in the temple service get their food from the temple, and those who serve at the altar share in what is sacrificed on the altar? In the same way, the Lord commanded that those who proclaim the gospel should get their living by the gospel.[73]

1 Tim. 5:18. for the scripture says, "You shall not muzzle an ox while it is treading out the grain," and, "The laborer deserves to be paid."

---

[73] CEV: When we told the message to you, it was like planting spiritual seed. So we have the right to accept material things as our harvest from you. If others have the right to do this, we have an even greater right. But we haven't used this right of ours. We are willing to put up with anything to keep from causing trouble for the message about Christ. Don't you know that people who work in the temple make their living from what is brought to the temple? Don't you know that a person who serves at the altar is given part of what is offered? In the same way, the Lord wants everyone who preaches the good news to make a living from preaching this message.

Q. These scriptures indicate that there is an obligation upon the believers to help with material things those who minister to them; just as they truly minister spiritual things to the flock. But this seems to be voluntary. Therefore shouldn't true ministers preach, whether or not they are certain of such support? What does the apostle say about himself on this matter? And how does he advise others?

A. *1 Cor. 9:15-18.* But I have made no use of any of these rights, nor am I writing this so that they may be applied in my case. Indeed, I would rather die than that—no one will deprive me of my ground for boasting! If I proclaim the gospel, this gives me no ground for boasting, for an obligation is laid on me, and woe to me if I do not proclaim the gospel! For if I do this of my own will, I have a reward; but if not of my own will, I am entrusted with a commission. What then is my reward? Just this: that in my proclamation I may make the gospel free of charge, so as not to make full use of my rights in the gospel.

Acts 20:33-35. I coveted no one's silver or gold or clothing. You know for yourselves that I worked with my own hands to support myself and my companions. In all this I have given you an example that by such work we must support the weak, remembering the words of the Lord Jesus, for he himself said, "It is more blessed to give than to receive."

Q. The apostle frequently indicates that one qualification for teachers is that they not be motivated by money. What then are we to think of those teachers who will not preach without being paid? Who, in fact, will acquire forced maintenance from those who receive no spiritual ministry from them? Are they like the ministers of Christ? Or how otherwise does scripture speak of them?[74]

A. *Isa. 56:11.* The dogs have a mighty appetite; they never have enough. The shepherds also have no understanding; they have all turned to their own way, to their own gain, one and all.[75]

---

[74] In Barclay's time pastors were appointed public officials, paid from state funds, and for some of them the ministry was just a job, not a divine calling. The Quaker awakening contributed to the rise of the free church tradition, in which a freely chosen ministry is supported by voluntary contributions of believers rather than by taxation.

[75] CEV: You stupid leaders are a pack of hungry and greedy dogs that never get enough. You are shepherds who mistreat your own sheep for selfish gain.

Ezek. 34:2-3, 8. Mortal, prophesy against the shepherds of Israel: prophesy, and say to them—to the shepherds: Thus says the Lord GOD: "Ah, you shepherds of Israel who have been feeding yourselves! Should not shepherds feed the sheep? You eat the fat, you clothe yourselves with the wool, you slaughter the fatlings; but you do not feed the sheep." "As I live," says the Lord God, "because my sheep have become a prey, and my sheep have become food for all the wild animals, since there was no shepherd; and because my shepherds have not searched for my sheep, but the shepherds have fed themselves, and have not fed my sheep."

Micah 3:5, 11. Thus says the Lord concerning the prophets who lead my people astray, who cry "Peace" when they have something to eat, but declare war against those who put nothing into their mouths….Its rulers give judgment for a bribe, its priests teach for a price, its prophets give oracles for money; yet they lean upon the Lord and say, "Surely the Lord is with us! No harm shall come upon us."

Q. These are very clear testimonies from the Old Testament prophets! Are there similar statements by the apostles?

A. *1 Tim. 6:5-10.* …and wrangling among those who are depraved in mind and bereft of the truth, imagining that Godliness is a means of gain. Of course, there is great gain in Godliness combined with contentment; for we brought nothing into the world, so that we can take nothing out of it; but if we have food and clothing, we will be content with these. But those who want to be rich fall into temptation and are trapped by many senseless and harmful desires that plunge people into ruin and destruction. For the love of money is a root of all kinds of evil, and in their eagerness to be rich some have wandered away from the faith and pierced themselves with many pains.[76]

2 Tim. 3:2. For people will be lovers of themselves, lovers of money, boasters, arrogant, abusive, disobedient to their parents, ungrateful, unholy,

Titus 1:10. There are also many rebellious people, idle talkers and deceivers….

---

[76] REB: And endless wrangles—all typical of those whose minds are corrupted and have lost their grip of the truth. They think religion should yield dividends; and of course religion does yield high dividends, but only to those who are content with what they have. We brought nothing into this world, and we can take nothing out; if we have food and clothing let us rest content. Those who want to be rich fall into temptation and snares and into many foolish and harmful desires which plunge people into ruin and destruction. The love of money is the root of all evil, and in pursuit of it some have wandered from the faith and spiked themselves on many a painful thorn.

2 Pet. 2:1-3, 14-15. But false prophets also arose among the people, just as there will be false teachers among you, who will secretly bring in destructive opinions. They will even deny the Master who bought them—bringing swift destruction on themselves. Even so, many will follow their licentious ways, and because of these teachers the way of truth will be maligned. And in their greed they will exploit you with deceptive words. Their condemnation, pronounced against them long ago, has not been idle, and their destruction is not asleep....They have eyes full of adultery, insatiable for sin. They entice unsteady souls. They have hearts trained in greed. Accursed children! They have left the straight road and have gone astray, following the road of Balaam son of Bosor, who loved the wages of doing wrong.[77]

Jude 11, 16. Woe to them! For they go the way of Cain, and abandon themselves to Balaam's error for the sake of gain, and perish in Korah's rebellion....These are grumblers and malcontents; they indulge their own lusts; they are bombastic in speech, flattering people to their own advantage.

Q. Should there be order in the church of God?

A. *1 Cor. 14:40.* ...all things should be done decently and in order.

Q. What good order is prescribed in the church concerning preachers? Is it proper for only one or two to speak? Or may more, if they are moved to do so?

A. *1 Cor. 14:30-31, 33.* If a revelation is made to someone else sitting nearby, let the first person be silent. For you can all prophesy one by one, so that all may learn and all be encouraged....for God is a God not of disorder but of peace (as in all the churches of the saints).

---

[77] REB: In the past there were also false prophets among the people, just as you will have false teachers among you. They will introduce their destructive views, disowning the very Master who redeemed them, and bringing swift destruction on their own heads. They will gain many adherents to their dissolute practices, through whom the way of truth will be brought into disrepute. In their greed for money they will trade on your credulity with sheer fabrications. But judgement has long been in preparation for them with unsleeping eyes....They have eyes for nothing but loose women, eyes never resting from sin. They lure the unstable to their ruin; experts in mercenary greed, God's curse is on them!

Q. Is there any promise that daughters as well as sons shall prophesy under the gospel?

A. *Joel 2:28.* Then afterward I will pour out my spirit on all flesh; your sons and your daughters shall prophesy, your old men shall dream dreams, and your young men shall see visions.

Q. Has this promise been fulfilled? And is it to be fulfilled further?

A. *Acts 2:16-17.* No, this is what was spoken through the prophet Joel: "In the last days it will be," God declares, "that I will pour out my Spirit upon all flesh, and your sons and your daughters shall prophesy, and your young men shall see visions, and your old men shall dream dreams."

Q. Is there any account in scripture of its happening?

A. *Acts 21:9.* [Philip] had four unmarried daughters who had the gift of prophecy.

Q. May all women speak? Or are some commanded to keep silence in the church?

A. *1 Cor. 14:33b-35.* As in all the churches of the saints women should be silent in the churches. For they are not permitted to speak, but should be subordinate, as the law also says. If there is anything they desire to know, let them ask their husbands at home. For it is shameful for a woman to speak in church.[78]

1 Tim. 2:11-12. Let a woman learn in silence with full submission. I permit no woman to teach or to have authority over a man; she is to keep silent.[79]

---

[78] NJerB: As in all the churches of God's holy people, women are to remain quiet in the assemblies, since they have no permission to speak: theirs is a subordinate part, as the Law itself says. If there is anything they want to know, they should ask their husbands at home: it is shameful for a woman to speak in the assembly.

[79] NJerB has: During instruction, a woman should be quiet and respectful. I give no permission for a woman to teach or to have authority over a man. A woman ought to be quiet.

Q. The first of these citations seems to relate only to women who have husbands. What about unmarried women? The second passage is not said about the church, but only that a woman ought not to usurp authority over a man. Does this have any limitation? Doesn't the same apostle give directions on how women who speak should behave in church?

A. *1 Cor. 11:4-5.* Any man who prays or prophesies with something on his head disgraces his head, but any woman who prays or prophesies with her head unveiled disgraces her head—it is one and the same thing as having her head shaved.[80]

---

[80] Early Friends insisted on the right of women to participate in ministry, as noted in the scriptures cited, but sought to channel such ministry within bounds of accepted social propriety. For a time Quakers held separate men's and women's business meetings, as a sort of middle course to maximize freedom within cultural boundaries. As noted later in regard to passages in the *Confession* about social relationships, it was reciprocal respect under the Lordship of Jesus Christ, the present Teacher, that was the Quaker concern.

Chapter Ten

Worship

Q. What kind of worship is acceptable to God?

A. *John 4:23-24.* But the hour is coming, and is now here, when the true worshipers will worship the Father in spirit and truth, for the Father seeks such as these to worship him. God is spirit, and those who worship him must worship in spirit and truth.[81]

Q. Inasmuch as prayer is part of worship, when should we pray?

A. *Luke 18:1.* Then Jesus told them a parable about their need to pray always and not to lose heart.

1 Thess. 5:17. Pray without ceasing.

Q. Does God esteem a particular way of calling upon him?

A. *Rom. 10:12.* For there is no distinction between Jew and Greek; the same Lord is Lord of all and is generous to all who call on him.

Q. Does God hear the prayers of all who call upon him?

A. *Ps. 145:18.* The Lord is near to all who call on him, to all who call on him in truth.[82]

Prov. 15:29. The Lord is far from the wicked, but he hears the prayer of the righteous.

John 9:31. We know that God does not listen to sinners, but he does listen to one who worships him and obeys his will.

---

[81] CEV: But a time is coming, and it is already here! Even now the true worshipers are being led by the Spirit to worship the Father according to the truth. These are the ones the Father is seeking to worship him. God is Spirit, and those who worship God must be led by the Spirit to worship him according to the truth.

[82] CEV: ...and you (our Lord) are near to everyone whose prayers are sincere.

1 John 5:14. And this is the boldness we have in him, that if we ask anything according to his will, he hears us.[83]

Q. In what way does the apostle declare that he will pray?

A. *1 Cor. 14:15.* What should I do then? I will pray with the spirit, but I will pray with the mind also; I will sing praise with the spirit, but I will sing praise with the mind also.

Q. Must we always pray in the Spirit?

A. *Eph. 6:18.* Pray in the Spirit at all times in every prayer and supplication. To that end keep alert and always persevere in supplication for all the saints.[84]

Q. Since we are commanded always to pray in the Spirit, are we unable to pray by ourselves without the help of the Spirit?

A. *Rom. 8:26-27.* Likewise the Spirit helps us in our weakness; for we do not know how to pray as we ought, but that very Spirit intercedes with sighs too deep for words. And God, who searches the heart, knows what is the mind of the Spirit, because the Spirit intercedes for the saints according to the will of God.[85]

Q. Apparently prayers are worthless when offered without the leading and help of the Spirit. Are there really any spiritual things a person can do without the assistance of the Spirit?

---

[83] NIV: We have this assurance in approaching God, that if we ask anything according to his will, he hears us.

[84] TEV: Do all this in prayer, asking for God's help. Pray on every occasion, as the Spirit leads. For this reason keep alert and never give up; pray always for all of God's people.

[85] TEV: In the same way the Spirit also comes to help us, weak that we are. For we do not know how we ought to pray; the Spirit himself pleads with God for us, in groans that words cannot express. And God, who sees into the hearts of men, knows what the thought of the Spirit is; because the Spirit pleads with God on behalf of his people and in accordance with his will.

A. *1 Cor. 12:3.* Therefore I want you to understand that no one speaking by the Spirit of God ever says "Let Jesus be cursed!" and no one can say "Jesus is Lord" except by the Holy Spirit.[86]

Q. This is strange! The Spirit seems more essential than many nominal Christians suppose. Some of them can scarcely give a good account of whether they have the Spirit or not. However if some say things that are true, are they not true even though spoken without the Spirit's aid?

A. *Jer. 5:2.* Although they say, "As the Lord lives," yet they swear falsely.

Q. From all of these scriptures it is apparent that true worship of God is in the Spirit. And, since worship is not limited to a certain place, or a certain time, what are we to think of those who plead for observation of certain days?

A. *Gal. 4:9-11.* Now, however, that you have come to know God, or rather to be known by God, how can you turn back again to the weak and beggarly elemental spirits? How can you want to be enslaved to them again? You are observing special days, and months, and seasons, and years. I am afraid that my work for you may have been wasted.

Col. 2:16-17. Therefore do not let anyone condemn you in matters of food and drink or of observing festivals, new moons, or Sabbaths. These are only a shadow of what is to come, but the substance belongs to Christ.[87]

Q. If this is the case, may not some Christians lawfully esteem all days alike, while others esteem certain days above others? What rule does the apostle give in this case?

A. *Rom. 14:5-6.* Some judge one day to be better than another, while others judge all days to be alike. Let all be fully convinced in their own minds. Those who observe the day, observe it in honor of the Lord. Also those who eat, eat in honor of the Lord, since they give thanks to God; while those who abstain, abstain in honor of the Lord and give thanks to God.

---

[86] CEV: Now I want you to know that if you are led by God's Spirit, you will say that Jesus is Lord, and you will never curse Jesus.

[87] TEV: So let no one make rules about what you eat or drink, or about the subject of holy days, or the new moon festival, or the Sabbath.

Q. But is it not convenient and necessary for a day to be set apart to meet and worship God? Didn't the apostles and early Christians meet on the first day of the week to take up their collections and to worship?

A. *1 Cor. 16:1-2.* Now concerning the collection for the saints: you should follow the directions I gave to the churches of Galatia. On the first day of every week, each of you is to put aside and save whatever extra you earn, so that collections need not be taken when I come.

Chapter Eleven

Baptism, Bread and Wine

Q. How many baptisms are there?

A. *Eph. 4:5.* One Lord, one faith, one baptism.

Q. What is this baptism?

A. *1 Pet. 3:21-22.* And baptism, which this prefigured, now saves you—not as a removal of dirt from the body, but as an appeal to God for a good conscience, through the resurrection of Jesus Christ, who has gone into heaven and is at the right hand of God, with angels, authorities, and powers made subject to him.[88]

Q. What does John the Baptist say about Christ's baptism? How does he distinguish it from his own?

A. *Matt. 3:11.* I baptize you with water for repentance, but one who is more powerful than I is coming after me; I am not worthy to carry his sandals. He will baptize you with the Holy Spirit and fire.

Q. Doesn't Christ make the same distinction?

A. *Acts 1:4-5.* While staying with them, he ordered them not to leave Jerusalem, but to wait there for the promise of the Father. "This," he said, "is what you have heard from me; for John baptized with water, but you will be baptized with the Holy Spirit not many days from now."

---

[88] NJerB: It is the baptism corresponding to this water which saves you now—not the washing off of physical dirt but the pledge of a good conscience given to God through the resurrection of Jesus Christ, who has entered heaven and is at God's right hand, with angels, ruling forces and powers subject to him.

Q. Doesn't the apostle Peter also observe this?

A. *Acts 11:15-16.* And as I began to speak, the Holy Spirit fell upon them just as it had upon us at the beginning. And I remembered the word of the Lord, how he had said, "John baptized with water, but you will be baptized with the Holy Spirit."

Q. Apparently John's baptism must pass away in order for Christ's to increase.

A. *John 3:30.* He must increase, but I must decrease.

Q. It would seem then that many may be sprinkled with and dipped in water and yet not be truly baptized with the baptism of Christ. What are the real effects in those who are truly baptized with the baptism of Christ?

A. *Rom. 6:3-4.* Do you not know that all of us who have been baptized into Christ Jesus were baptized into his death? Therefore we have been buried with him by baptism into death, so that, just as Christ was raised from the dead by the glory of the Father, so we too might walk in newness of life.

Gal. 3:27. As many of you as were baptized into Christ have clothed yourselves with Christ.[89]

Col. 2:12. When you were buried with him in baptism, you were also raised with him through faith in the power of God, who raised him from the dead.

Q. It would seem that there was a baptism of water, which was John's baptism, which John the Baptist himself distinguished from that of Christ. Didn't something similar pertain to the eating of bread and drinking of wine appointed by Christ for his disciples to remember him?

A. *1 Cor. 11:23-25.* For I received from the Lord what I also handed on to you, that the Lord Jesus on the night when he was betrayed took a loaf of bread, and when he had given thanks, he broke it and said, "This is my body that is for you. Do this in remembrance of me." In the same way he took the cup also, after supper, saying, "This cup is the new covenant in my blood. Do this, as often as you drink it, in remembrance of me."

---

[89] TEV: You were baptized into union with Christ, and so have taken upon yourselves the qualities of Christ himself.

Q. How long was this to continue?

A. *1 Cor. 11:26.* For as often as you eat this bread and drink the cup, you proclaim the Lord's death until he comes.[90]

Q. Did Christ promise to come again to his disciples?

A. *John 14:18, 23.* "I will not leave you orphaned; I am coming to you...." Jesus answered him [Judas, not Iscariot], "Those who love me will keep my word, and my Father will love them, and we will come to them and make our home with them."

Q. Was this to be an inward coming?

A. *John 14:20.* On that day you will know that I am in my Father, and you in me, and I in you.

Q. Apparently this was even reflected in the practice of the church of Corinth. After Christ had come again inwardly, were there certain appointed acts which were positively commanded and zealously and conscientiously practiced by the saints of old, which were not to be of perpetual continuance, and which no longer need to be practiced in the church?

A. *John 13:14-15.* So if I, your Lord and Teacher, have washed your feet, you also ought to wash one another's feet. For I have set you an example, that you also should do as I have done to you.

Acts 15:28-29. For it has seemed good to the Holy Spirit and to us to impose on you no further burden than these essentials: that you abstain from what has been sacrificed to idols and from blood and from what is strangled and from fornication. If you keep yourselves from these, you will do well.

James 5:14. Are any among you sick? They should call for the elders of the church and have them pray over them, anointing them with oil in the name of the Lord.

---

[90] NJerB: *Whenever* you eat this bread, then, and drink this cup, you are proclaiming the Lord's death until he comes.

Q. These commands are no less positive than the other ones. Indeed, some commands were asserted as essential to a Spirit-guided life and no less important than abstaining from sexual immorality. Yet most Protestants have laid aside these practices as not needing to be perpetuated. What other scriptures indicate specifically that bread and wine rituals need not continue?

A. *Rom. 14:17.* For the kingdom of God is not food and drink but righteousness and peace and joy in the Holy Spirit.[91]

Col. 2:16, 20-22. Therefore do not let anyone condemn you in matters of food and drink or of observing festivals, new moons, or sabbaths....If with Christ you died to the elemental spirits of the universe, why do you live as if you still belonged to the world? Why do you submit to regulations, "Do not handle, Do not taste, Do not touch"? All these regulations refer to things that perish with use; they are simply human commands and teachings.

Q. These scriptures speak as plainly for abolishing these things as for continuing them. What, then, is the bread with which believers are to be nourished?

A. *John 6:32-35.* Then Jesus said to them, "Very truly, I tell you, it was not Moses who gave you the bread from heaven, but it is my Father who gives you the true bread from heaven. For the bread of God is that which comes down from heaven and gives life to the world." They said to him, "Sir, give us this bread always." Jesus said to them, "I am the bread of life. Whoever comes to me will never be hungry, and whoever believes in me will never be thirsty."

John 6:48-58. "I am the bread of life. Your ancestors ate the manna in the wilderness, and they died. This is the bread that comes down from heaven, so that one may eat of it and not die. I am the living bread that came down from heaven. Whoever eats of this bread will live forever; and the bread that I will give for the life of the world is my flesh." The Jews then disputed among themselves, saying, "How can this man give us his flesh to eat?" So Jesus said to them, "Very truly, I tell you, unless you eat the flesh of the Son of Man and drink his blood, you have no life

---

[91] CEV: God's kingdom isn't about eating and drinking. It is about pleasing God, about living in peace, and about true happiness. All this comes from the Holy Spirit.

in you. Those who eat my flesh and drink my blood have eternal life, and I will raise them up on the last day; for my flesh is true food and my blood is true drink. Those who eat my flesh and drink my blood abide in me, and I in them. Just as the living Father sent me, and I live because of the Father, so whoever eats me will live because of me. This is the bread that came down from heaven, not like that which your ancestors ate, and they died. But the one who eats this bread will live forever."

Chapter Twelve

The Life of a Christian

Q. What is true religion?

A. *James 1:27.* Religion that is pure and undefiled before God, the Father, is this: to care for orphans and widows in their distress, and to keep oneself unstained by the world.

Q. What is required of us?

A. *Micah 6:8.* He has told you, O mortal, what is good; and what does the Lord require of you but to do justice, and to love kindness, and to walk humbly with your God?

Isa. 66:2b. But this is the one to whom I will look, to the humble and contrite in spirit, who trembles at my word.

Q. Does God require people to be quakers, that is, to tremble at his word? Were there any among the ancient believers who did so?

A. *Ezra 9:4.* Then all who trembled at the words of the God of Israel....[92]

Ezra 10:3. So now let us make a covenant with our God to send away all these wives and their children, according to the counsel of my Lord and of those who tremble at the commandment of our God.

---

[92] NAB renders this: Around me gathered all who were in dread of the sentence of the God of Israel.

[NOTE] Barclay exhibits a wry sense of humor by giving Scriptural support to a nickname "quaker" first used derisively against Friends. He has turned ridicule into a testimony of biblical faithfulness. George Fox had earlier acted similarly, by urging prosecuting authorities to "tremble and quake" at the word of the Lord. A more recent bit of Friends' humor is: "What was the longest Quaker meeting on record?" Answer: "When Job sat silently for seven days and seven nights with his friends."

Q. Ezra apparently loved and had a high opinion of quakers, since he would have their counsel followed! Do any of the other prophets point to quakers or tremblers as God's people?

A. *Isa. 66:5* Hear the word of the Lord, you who tremble at his word: Your own people who hate you and reject you for my name's sake have said, "Let the Lord be glorified, so that we may see your joy"; but it is they who shall be put to shame.

Jer. 33:9. And this city shall be to me a name of joy, a praise and a glory before all the nations of the earth who shall hear of all the good that I do for them; they shall fear and tremble because of all the good and all the prosperity I provide for it.

Q. The prophets promised good things to quakers. What happens to those who do not tremble and quake?

A. *Jer. 5:21-22.* Hear this, O foolish and senseless people, who have eyes, but do not see, who have ears, but do not hear. Do you not fear me? says the Lord; Do you not tremble before me?

Q. Are then all God's children quakers? And are we commanded to quake or tremble in order to be saved, both under the law, and now under the gospel?

A. *Ps. 2:11.* Serve the Lord with fear, with trembling.[93]

Dan. 6:26a. I make a decree, that in all my royal dominion people should tremble and fear before the God of Daniel: For he is the living God, enduring forever.

Phil. 2:12. ...work out your own salvation with fear and trembling.[94]

Q. What are the chief commandments?

A. *Matt. 22:37-40.* He said to him, "'You shall love the Lord your God with all your heart, and with all your soul, and with all your mind.' This is the greatest and first commandment. And a second is like it: 'You shall love your neighbor as yourself.' On these two commandments hang all the law and the prophets."

---

[93] CEV: Serve and honor the Lord; be glad and tremble.
[94] CEV: ...work with fear and trembling to discover what it really means to be saved.

Q. What should a Christian seek first?

A. *Matt. 6:33.* But strive first for the kingdom of God and his righteousness, and all these things will be given to you as well.

Q. How should Christians behave themselves in this world?

A. *1 Cor. 7:29-31.* I mean, brothers and sisters, the appointed time has grown short; from now on, let even those who have wives be as though they had none, and those who mourn as though they were not mourning, and those who rejoice as though they were not rejoicing, and those who buy as though they had no possessions, and those who deal with the world as though they had no dealings with it. For the present form of this world is passing away.[95]

Q. What does the apostle add about appropriate behavior for Christian men and women?

A. *1 Tim. 2:8-10.* I desire, then, that in every place the men should pray, lifting up holy hands without anger or argument; also that the women should dress themselves modestly and decently in suitable clothing, not with their hair braided, or with gold, pearls, or expensive clothes, but with good works, as is proper for women who profess reverence for God.[96]

---

[95] CEV: My dear friends, what I mean is that the Lord will soon come, and it won't matter if you are married or not. It will be all the same if you are crying or laughing, or if you are buying or are completely broke. It won't make any difference how much good you are getting from this world, or how much you like it. This world as we know it is now passing away.

[96] Phillips reads: Therefore, I want the men to pray in all the churches with sincerity, without resentment or doubt in their minds. Similarly, the women should be dressed neatly, their adornment being modesty and serious-mindedness. It is not for them to have an elaborate hairstyle, jewelry of gold or pearls, or expensive clothes, but, as becomes women who profess to believe in God, it is for them to show their faith by the way they live.

Q. The apostle Paul strongly opposes vanity and superfluous clothing among Christians. What does the apostle Peter say about this?

A. *1 Pet. 3:3-4.* Do not adorn yourselves outwardly by braiding your hair, and by wearing gold ornaments or fine clothing; rather, let your adornment be the inner self with the lasting beauty of a gentle and quiet spirit, which is very precious in God's sight.[97]

Q. Peter is clear on this point. But on another issue, what does scripture say about respect for persons among Christians?

A. *James 2:1-9.* My brothers and sisters, do you with your acts of favoritism really believe in our glorious Lord Jesus Christ? For if a person with gold rings and in fine clothes comes into your assembly, and if a poor person in dirty clothes also comes in, and if you take notice of the one wearing the fine clothes and say, "Have a seat here, please," while to the one who is poor you say, "Stand there," or, "Sit at my feet," have you not made distinctions among yourselves, and become judges with evil thoughts? Listen, my beloved brothers and sisters. Has not God chosen the poor in the world to be rich in faith and to be heirs of the kingdom that he has promised to those who love him? But you have dishonored the poor. Is it not the rich who oppress you? Is it not they who drag you into court? Is it not they who blaspheme the excellent name that was invoked over you? You do well if you really fulfill the royal law according to the scripture, "You shall love your neighbor as yourself." But if you show partiality, you commit sin and are convicted by the law as transgressors.

---

[97] REB: Your beauty should lie, not in outward adornment—braiding the hair, wearing gold ornaments, or dressing up in fine clothes—but in the inmost self, with its imperishable quality of a gentle, quiet spirit, which is of high value in the sight of God.

Q. This should be sufficient reproof for ranking Christians by economic status or birth. However, shouldn't Christians respect social relationships, such as that between a master and a servant? What warning do the apostles give in this case?[98]

A. *Eph. 6:5-9 [see also Col. 3:22-25; 4:1].* Slaves, obey your earthly masters with fear and trembling, in singleness of heart, as you obey Christ; not only while being watched, and in order to please them, but as slaves of Christ, doing the will of God from the heart. Render service with enthusiasm, as to the Lord and not to men and women, knowing that whatever good we do, we will receive the same again from the Lord, whether we are slaves or free. And, masters, do the same to them. Stop threatening them, for you know that both of you have the same Master in heaven, and with him there is no partiality.

---

[98] Barclay's biblical citations about slavery may seem puzzling to modern readers, aware of historic efforts by Quakers to abolish slavery, and mindful of the strong witness against human bondage by John Woolman and John Greenleaf Whittier. Early Quakers read the New Testament passages cited below as Paul's first readers would have, as supporting institutional social order in respect to work and family, and looking for the leaven of the Gospel to effect social change nonviolently. The book of Philemon, the example of Jesus, and the admonition of James (the preceding reference), reinforced this expectation. Although the views of Barclay seem somewhat paternalistic, the context should be noted. First, early Friends read these pastoral admonitions in the King James version, which used the social pairing of "servants" and "masters," as well as "children" and "parents", and "husbands" and "wives." Second, they honored Christ as present Lord and master over all persons, whatever their station in life. Third, many British households, in addition to upper class Quakers such as Barclay and William Penn, had servants, and so these admonitions for reciprocal respect constituted practical advice. Fourth, Quaker transcendence of class distinctions became evident by the fact that household servants became endorsed ministers of the Gospel, e.g., Jan Waugh, and Richard and Anne Cleaton. Fifth, when the nature of the bondage exhibited by the enslavement of African people became evident, Quakers were early and persistent advocates for its abolition. About the time Barclay wrote the *Catechism*, George Fox had admonished New World families to treat African slaves as a sort of extended family, equally valued in the sight of God. But others at this time, such as George Keith and William Edmundson, were more acutely aware of the distinction between indentured servants and merchandized slaves. They publicly attacked the latter as immoral. In 1688 Francis Daniel Pastorius, and Abraham up Den graef authored a Mennonite-Quaker minute, addressed to Germantown (Pennsylvania) Monthly Meeting, calling graphic attention to the immorality of stealing people from their families and selling them abroad. During the next seventy years Quaker yearly meetings led the Christian abolitionist movement.

1 Tim. 6:1-2. Let all who are under the yoke of slavery regard their masters as worthy of all honor, so that the name of God and the teaching may not be blasphemed. Those who have believing masters must not be disrespectful to them on the ground that they are members of the church; rather they must serve them all the more, since those who benefit by their service are believers and beloved. Teach and urge these duties.

Titus 2:9-10. Tell slaves to be submissive to their masters and to give satisfaction in every respect; they are not to talk back, not to pilfer, but to show complete and perfect fidelity, so that in everything they may be an ornament to the doctrine of God our Savior.[99]

1 Pet. 2:18-21. Slaves, accept the authority of your masters with all deference, not only those who are kind and gentle but also those who are harsh. For it is a credit to you if, being aware of God, you endure pain while suffering unjustly. If you endure when you are beaten for doing wrong, what credit is that? But if you endure when you do right and suffer for it, you have God's approval. For to this you have been called, because Christ also suffered for you, leaving you an example, so that you should follow in his steps.

Q. What good advice do the scriptures give regarding the relationship between parents and children?

A. *Eph. 6:1-4.* Children, obey your parents in the Lord, for this is right. "Honor your father and mother"—this is the first commandment with a promise: "so that it may be well with you and you may live long on the earth." And, fathers, do not provoke your children to anger, but bring them up in the discipline and instruction of the Lord.

Col. 3:20-21. Children, obey your parents in everything, for this is your acceptable duty in the Lord. Fathers, do not provoke your children, or they may lose heart.

---

[99] NJerB has: Slaves must be obedient to their masters in everything, and do what is wanted without argument; and there must be no pilfering—they must show complete honesty at all times, so that they are in every way a credit to the teaching of God our Saviour.

Q. What about the relationship between husbands and wives?[100]

A. *Eph. 5:22-25, 28, 31, 33.* Wives, be subject to your husbands as you are to the Lord. For the husband is the head of the wife just as Christ is the head of the church, the body of which he is the Savior. Just as the church is subject to Christ, so also wives ought to be, in everything, to their husbands. Husbands, love your wives, just as Christ loved the church and gave himself up for her....In the same way, husbands should love their wives as they do their own bodies. He who loves his wife loves himself...." For this reason a man will leave his father and mother and be joined to his wife, and the two will become one flesh." ...Each of you, however, should love his wife as himself, and a wife should respect her husband.[101]

Col. 3:19. Husbands, love your wives and never treat them harshly.

1 Pet. 3:1, 2, 7. Wives, in the same way, accept the authority of your husbands, so that, even if some of them do not obey the word, they may be won over without a word by their wives' conduct, when they see the purity and reverence of your lives. Husbands, in the same way, show consideration for your wives in your life together, paying honor to the woman as the weaker sex, since they too are also heirs of the gracious gift of life—so that nothing may hinder your prayers.

---

[100] As noted above, about servants and masters, the following passages are admonitions for reciprocal respect, in the context of all being under the Lordship of Jesus Christ, the present Teacher, whatever the constraints of social order. From the beginning Quakers acknowledged that not only servants could minister as well as masters, but women as well as men, and in some cases children as well as adults. What counted was the anointing of the Lord and the endorsement of the church. Margaret Fell Fox, "gentlewoman," was a leading minister. So was Mary Fisher, "servant," and several members of an early evangelistic band, the "Valiant Sixty."

[101] NJerB: Wives should be subject to their husbands as to the Lord, since as Christ is head of the Church and saves the whole body, so is a husband the head of his wife; and as the Church is subject to Christ, so should wives be to their husbands, in everything. Husbands should love their wives, just as Christ loved the Church and sacrificed himself for her....In the same way, husbands must love their wives as they love their own bodies; for a man to love his wife is for him to love himself....This is why a man leaves his father and mother and becomes attached to his wife, and the two become one flesh....To sum up, you also, each one of you, must love his wife as he loves himself; and let every wife respect her husband.

Q. What is the armor of a true Christian? And with what should they struggle?

A. *Eph. 6:11-17.* Put on the whole armor of God, so that you may be able to stand against the wiles of the devil. For our struggle is not against enemies of blood and flesh, but against the rulers, against the authorities, against the cosmic powers of this present darkness, against the spiritual forces of evil in the heavenly places. Therefore take up the whole armor of God, so that you may be able to withstand on that evil day, and having done everything, to stand firm. Stand therefore, and fasten the belt of truth around your waist, and put on the breastplate of righteousness. As shoes for your feet put on whatever will make you ready to proclaim the gospel of peace. With all of these, take the shield of faith, with which you will be able to quench all the flaming arrows of the evil one. Take the helmet of salvation, and the sword of the Spirit, which is the word of God.

Q. What are the Christian's weapons? What is their purpose?

A. *2 Cor. 10:3-5.* Indeed, we live as human beings, but we do not wage war according to human standards; for the weapons of our warfare are not merely human, but they have divine power to destroy strongholds. We destroy arguments and every proud obstacle raised up against the knowledge of God, and we take every thought captive to obey Christ.

Q. Should there be strife and envy among Christians?

A. *James 3:13-18.* Who is wise and understanding among you? Show by your good life that your works are done with gentleness born of wisdom. But if you have bitter envy and selfish ambition in your hearts, do not be boastful and false to the truth. Such wisdom does not come down from above, but is earthly, unspiritual, devilish. For where there is envy and selfish ambition, there will also be disorder and wickedness of every kind. But the wisdom from above is first pure, then peaceable, gentle, willing to yield, full of mercy and good fruits, without a trace of partiality or hypocrisy. And a harvest of righteousness is sown in peace for those who make peace.[102]

[102] CEV: Are any of you wise or sensible? Then show it by living right and by being humble and wise in everything you do. But if your heart is full of bitter jealousy and selfishness, don't brag or lie to cover up the truth. That kind of wisdom doesn't come from above. It is earthly and selfish and comes from the devil himself. Whenever people are jealous or selfish, they cause trouble and do all sorts of cruel things. But the wisdom that comes from above leads us to be pure, friendly, gentle, sensible, kind, helpful, genuine and sincere. When peacemakers plant seeds of peace, they will harvest justice.

Q. Should wars be fought among Christians? What causes wars?

A. *James 4:1-2.* Those conflicts and disputes among you, where do they come from? Do they not come from your cravings that are at war within you? You want something and do not have it; so you commit murder. And you covet something and cannot obtain it; so you engage in disputes and conflicts. You do not have, because you do not ask.

Q. What does Christ say even about defensive war?

A. *Matt. 5:39.* But I say to you, Do not resist an evildoer. But if anyone strikes you on the right cheek, turn the other also;

Luke 6:27-29. But I say to you that listen, love your enemies, do good to those who hate you, bless those who curse you, pray for those who abuse you. If anyone strikes you on the cheek, offer the other also; and from anyone who takes away your coat do not withhold even your shirt.

Q. What do the apostles say?

A. *Rom. 12:17.* Do not repay anyone evil for evil, but take thought for what is noble in the sight of all.

1 Pet. 3:9. Do not repay evil for evil or abuse for abuse; but, on the contrary, repay with a blessing. It is for this that you were called—that you might inherit a blessing.

1 Thess. 5:15. See that none of you repays evil for evil, but always seek to do good to one another and to all.[103]

Q. In ancient times it was lawful to swear; and a confirming oath was then considered a way to end strife. Is it lawful also for Christians to swear?

A. *Matt. 5:33-37.* Again, you have heard that it was said to those of ancient times, "You shall not swear falsely, but carry out the vows you have made to the Lord." But I say to you, "Do not swear at all, either by heaven, for it is the throne of God, or by the earth, for it is his footstool,

---

[103] NJerB: Make sure that people do not try to repay evil for evil; always aim at what is best for each other and for everyone.

or by Jerusalem, for it is the city of the great King. And do not swear by your head, for you cannot make one hair white or black. Let your word be 'Yes, Yes' or 'No, No'; anything more than this comes from the evil one."

James 5:12. Above all, my beloved, do not swear, either by heaven or by earth or by any other oath, but let your "Yes" be yes and your "No" be no, so that you may not fall under condemnation.[104]

Q. Is it appropriate for Christians or believers to receive worldly honor from each other?

A. *John 5:44.* How can you believe when you accept glory from one another and do not seek the glory that comes from the one who alone is God?

Q. Does God allow us to give flattering titles to people?

A. *Job 32:21-22.* I will not show partiality to any person or use flattery toward anyone. For I do not know how to flatter—or my Maker would soon put an end to me!

Q. What should we say to those who quarrel with us for speaking, as appropriate, words such as "thou" to one person and "you" to many, which was Christ's and the believers' language in scripture?

A. *1 Tim. 6:3-4.* Whoever teaches otherwise and does not agree with the sound words of our Lord Jesus Christ and the teaching that is in accordance with Godliness, is conceited, understanding nothing, and has a morbid craving for controversy and for disputes about words. From these come envy, dissension, slander, base suspicions....

2 Tim. 1:13. Hold to the standard of sound teaching that you have heard from me, in the faith and love that are in Christ Jesus.

Q. What is the great commandment that Christ gave to his disciples, which defines them as disciples, and is urged by his apostles as well?

A. *John 13:34-35.* "I give you a new commandment, that you love one another. Just as I have loved you, you also should love one another. By this everyone will know that you are my disciples, if you have love for one another."

---

[104] NAB: But above all, my brothers, do not swear, either by heaven or by earth or with any other oath, but let your "Yes" mean "Yes" and your "No" mean "No," that you may not incur condemnation.

John 15:12, 17. This is my commandment, that you love one another as I have loved you....I am giving you these commands so that you may love one another.

Eph. 5:1-2. Therefore be imitators of God, as beloved children, and live in love, as Christ loved us and gave himself up for us, a fragrant offering and sacrifice to God.[105]

1 John 4:20-21. Those who say, "I love God," and hate their brothers or sisters, are liars; for those who do not love a brother or sister whom they have seen, cannot love God whom they have not seen. The commandment we have from him is this: those who love God must love their brothers and sisters also.

Q. Is humility important for Christians? What must we become like before we can enter into the kingdom?

A. *Matt. 18:3-4.* [Jesus] said, "Truly I tell you, unless you change and become like children, you will never enter the kingdom of heaven. Whoever becomes humble like this child is the greatest in the kingdom of heaven."

Q. Should Christians lord it over one another? What rule does Christ give in this case?

A. *Matt. 20:25-28.* But Jesus called them to him and said, "You know that the rulers of the Gentiles lord it over them, and their great ones are tyrants over them. It will not be so among you; but whoever wishes to be great among you must be your servant, and whoever wishes to be first among you must be your slave; just as the Son of Man came not to be served, but to serve and to give his life a ransom for many."

Q. What are the circumstances of Christians in this world?

A. *Matt. 10:16.* See, I am sending you out like sheep into the midst of wolves; so be wise as serpents and innocent as doves.

Luke 10:3. Go on your way. See, I am sending you out like lambs into the midst of wolves.

---

[105] CEV: Do as God does. After all, you are his dear children. Let love be your guide. Christ loved us and offered his life for us as a sacrifice that pleases God.

Q. Are we to expect afflictions and persecutions?

A. *Matt. 10:22 (id. Mark 13:13).* ...and you will be hated by all because of my name. But the one who endures to the end will be saved.

Luke 21:17. You will be hated by all because of my name.

John 15:18. "If the world hates you, be aware that it hated me before it hated you. If you belonged to the world, the world would love you as its own. Because you do not belong to the world, but I have chosen you out of the world—therefore the world hates you.

John 16:33. I have said this to you, so that in me you may have peace. In the world you face persecution. But take courage; I have conquered the world!

2 Tim. 3:12. Indeed, all who want to live a Godly life in Christ Jesus will be persecuted.[106]

Q. Should we fear persecution?

A. *Matt. 10:28.* Do not fear those who kill the body but cannot kill the soul; rather fear him who can destroy both soul and body in hell.

Luke 12:4-5. I tell you, my friends, do not fear those who kill the body, and after that can do nothing more. But I will warn you whom to fear: fear him who, after he has killed, has authority to cast into hell. Yes, I tell you, fear him!

Q. Of what advantage is it to suffer persecution cheerfully, and what is the hazard for those who shun it?

A. *Matt. 5:10.* Blessed are those who are persecuted for righteousness' sake, for theirs is the kingdom of heaven.[107]

1 Pet. 3:14. But even if you do suffer for doing what is right, you are blessed. Do not fear what they fear, and do not be intimidated.[108]

---

[106] CEV: Anyone who belongs to Christ Jesus and wants to live right will have trouble from others.

[107] CEV: God blesses those people who are treated badly for doing right. They belong to the kingdom of heaven.

[108] CEV: Even if you have to suffer for doing good things, God will bless you. So stop being afraid and don't worry about what people might do.

Matt. 10:32-33. Everyone therefore who acknowledges me before others, I also will acknowledge before my Father in heaven; but whoever denies me before others, I also will deny before my Father in heaven.

Matt. 10:37-39. Whoever loves father or mother more than me is not worthy of me…and whoever does not take up the cross and follow me is not worthy of me. Those who find their life will lose it, and those who lose their life for my sake will find it.

Luke 12:8-9. And I tell you, everyone who acknowledges me before others, the Son of Man also will acknowledge before the angels of God; but whoever denies me before others will be denied before the angels of God.[109]

Matt. 16:24-25. Then Jesus told his disciples, "If any want to become my followers, let them deny themselves and take up their cross and follow me. For those who want to save their life will lose it, and those who lose their life for my sake will find it."[110]

2 Tim. 2:12. if we endure, we will also reign with him; if we deny him, he will also deny us;

Luke 14:26. Whoever comes to me and does not hate father and mother, wife and children, brothers and sisters, yes, and even life itself, cannot be my disciple

Luke 9:23-24. Then he said to them all, "If any want to become my followers, let them deny themselves and take up their cross daily and follow me. For those who want to save their life will lose it, and those who lose their life for my sake will save it."

Mark 8:34-35. He called the crowd with his disciples, and said to them, "If any want to become my followers, let them deny themselves and take up their cross and follow me. For those who want to save their life will lose it, and those who lose their life for my sake, and for the sake of the gospel, will save it."

---

[109] REB: I tell you this: whoever acknowledges me before others, the Son of Man will acknowledge before the angels of God; but whoever disowns me before others will be disowned before the angels of God.

[110] CEV: Then Jesus said to his disciples: "If any of you want to be my followers, you must forget about yourself. You must take up your cross and follow me. If you want to save your life, you will destroy it. But if you give up your life for me, you will find it."

Q. According to these scriptures nothing is more certain than that Christians must suffer persecution in this world, personally and materially. But shall they not also suffer as to their good names, being considered blasphemers, heretics, and deceivers?

A. *Matt. 10:24-25.* A disciple is not above the teacher, nor a slave above the master; it is enough for the disciple to be like the teacher, and the slave like the master. If they have called the master of the house Beelzebub, how much more will they malign those of his household![111]

Matt. 5:11. Blessed are you when people revile you and persecute you and utter all kinds of evil against you falsely on my account.

Acts 6:11-12. Then they secretly instigated some men to say, "We have heard him speak blasphemous words against Moses and God." They stirred up the people as well as the elders and the scribes; then they suddenly confronted him, seized him, and brought him before the council.

Acts 17:6. When they could not find them, they dragged Jason and some believers before the city authorities, shouting, "These people who have been turning the world upside down have come here also."

Acts 24:14. But this I admit to you, that according to the Way, which they call a sect, I worship the God of our ancestors, believing everything laid down according to the law or written in the prophets.

1 Cor. 4:13. When slandered, we speak kindly. We have become like the rubbish of the world, the dregs of all things, to this very day.[112]

2 Cor. 6:8. ...in honor and dishonor, in ill repute and good repute. We are treated as impostors, and yet are true.

Q. It is clear from what has been mentioned that Christians are to expect persecution and tribulation—that they are always to be the sheep and never the wolves, the persecuted and never the persecutors, the afflicted and never the afflicters, the reproached and never the reproachers. Is it not appropriate then

---

[111] REB: No pupil ranks above his teacher, no servant above his master. The pupil should be content to share his teacher's lot, the servant to share his master's. If the master has been called Beelzeboul, how much more his household!

[112] CEV: When someone curses us, we answer with kind words. Until now we are thought of as nothing more than the trash and garbage of this world.

for Christians—far from persecuting others—to pray for their persecutors? Is this Christ's command?

A. *Matt. 5:44.* But I say to you, Love your enemies and pray for those who persecute you,

Q. Was this Christ's own practice?

A. *Luke 23:34.* [Then Jesus said, "Father, forgive them, for they do not know what they are doing."] And they cast lots to divide his clothing.[113]

Q. In this is Christ to be our example?

A. *1 Pet. 2:21-23.* For to this you have been called, because Christ also suffered for you, leaving you an example, so that you should follow in his steps. He committed no sin, and no deceit was found in his mouth. When he was abused, he did not return abuse; when he suffered, he did not threaten; but he entrusted himself to the one who judges justly.

Q. Is there an instance in scripture of anyone who followed his example?

A. *Acts 7:60.* Then he [Stephen] knelt down and cried out in a loud voice, "Lord, do not hold this sin against them." When he had said this, he died.

Q. It appears from all of these scriptures that Christianity consists in exercising fear and trembling, humility, patience, and self-denial. What, then, are we to think of people whose religious devotion focuses on abstaining from marriage and certain foods, the worshiping of angels, and other similar acts of voluntary humility?

A. *1 Tim. 4:1-3.* Now the Spirit expressly says that in later times some will renounce the faith by paying attention to deceitful spirits and teachings of demons, through the hypocrisy of liars whose consciences are seared

---

[113] NSRV, NAB and CEV all bracket this verse and state that it is lacking in some ancient authorities.

with a hot iron. They forbid marriage and demand abstinence from foods, which God created to be received with thanksgiving by those who believe and know the truth.[114]

Col. 2:18. Do not let anyone disqualify you, insisting on self-abasement and worship of angels, dwelling on visions, puffed up without cause by a human way of thinking,

---

[114] CEV: God's Spirit clearly says that in the last days many people will turn from their faith. They will be fooled by evil spirits and by teachings that come from demons. They will also be fooled by the false claims of liars, whose consciences have lost all feeling. These liars will forbid people to marry or to eat certain foods. But God created these foods to be eaten with thankful hearts by his followers who know the truth.

Chapter Thirteen

Governance

Q. What is the duty of a one who governs?

A. *2 Sam. 23:3-4a.* The God of Israel has spoken, the Rock of Israel has said to me: One who rules over people justly, ruling in the fear of God, is like the light of morning....

Q. According to the scriptures, what is the duty of those who are under authority?

A. *Rom. 13:1-5.* Let every person be subject to the governing authorities; for there is no authority except from God, and those authorities that exist have been instituted by God. Therefore whoever resists authority resists what God has appointed, and those who resist will incur judgment. For rulers are not a terror to good conduct, but to bad. Do you wish to have no fear of the authority? Then do what is good, and you will receive its approval; for it is God's servant for your good. But if you do what is wrong, you should be afraid, for the authority does not bear the sword in vain! It is the servant of God to execute wrath on the wrongdoer. Therefore one must be subject, not only because of wrath but also because of conscience.[115]

1 Pet. 2:13-15. For the Lord's sake accept the authority of every human institution, whether of the emperor as supreme, or of governors, as sent

---

[115] CEV: Obey the rulers who have authority over you. Only God can give authority to anyone, and he puts these rulers in their places of power. People who oppose the authorities are opposing what God has done, and they will be punished. Rulers are a threat to evil people, not to good people. There is no need to be afraid of the authorities. Just do right, and they will praise you for it. After all, they are God's servants, and it is their duty to help you. If you do something wrong, you ought to be afraid, because these rulers have the right to punish you. They are God's servants who punish criminals to show how angry God is. But you should obey the rulers because you know it is the right thing to do, and not just because of God's anger.

by him to punish those who do wrong and to praise those who do right. For it is God's will that by doing right you should silence the ignorance of the foolish.[116]

Q. Ought taxes to be paid to them?

A. *Rom. 13:6-7.* For the same reason you also pay taxes, for the authorities are God's servants, busy with this very thing. Pay to all what is due them—taxes to whom taxes are due, revenue to whom revenue is due, respect to whom respect is due, honor to whom honor is due.

Matt. 22:21. Then he said to them, "Give therefore to the emperor the things that are the emperor's, and to God the things that are God's."

Q. Must we obey government officials in things that we are persuaded in our minds are contrary to the commands of Christ?

A. *Acts 4:18-20.* So they called them and ordered them not to speak or teach at all in the name of Jesus. But Peter and John answered them, "Whether it is right in God's sight to listen to you rather than to God, you must judge; for we cannot keep from speaking about what we have seen and heard."

Acts 5:27-29. When they had brought them, they had them stand before the council. The high priest questioned them, saying, "We gave you strict orders not to teach in this name, yet here you have filled Jerusalem with your teaching and you are determined to bring this man's blood on us." But Peter and the apostles answered, "We must obey God rather than any human authority."

Q. How should officials behave in such cases, according to the counsel of wise Gamaliel?

A. *Acts 5:34-35.* But a Pharisee in the council named Gamaliel, a teacher of the law, respected by all the people, stood up and ordered the men to be put outside for a short time. Then he said to them, "Fellow Israelites, consider carefully what you propose to do to these men...."

---

[116] Phillips: Obey every man-made authority for the Lord's sake—whether it be the emperor, as the supreme ruler, or the governors whom he has appointed to punish evil-doers and reward those who do good service. It is the will of God that you may thus silence the ill-informed criticisms of the foolish.

Acts 5:38-39 "...So in the present case, I tell you, keep away from these men and let them alone; because if this plan or this undertaking is of human origin, it will fail; but if it is of God, you will not be able to overthrow them—in that case you may even be found fighting against God."

Q. What gospel command does Christ give his people in this matter? How does he explain their duty?

A. *Matt. 13:27-29.* And the slaves of the householder came and said to him, "Master, did you not sow good seed in your field? Where, then, did these weeds come from?" He answered, "An enemy has done this." The slaves said to him, "Then do you want us to go and gather them?" But he replied, "No; for in gathering the weeds you would uproot the wheat along with them."

Q. Does Christ explain the tares as the wicked, whom the Godly must not cut off, lest by mistake they might harm the good? Instead leaving the sorting to God?

A. *Matt. 13:38-41.* The field is the world, and the good seed are the children of the kingdom; the weeds are the children of the evil one, and the enemy who sowed them is the devil; the harvest is the end of the age, and the reapers are angels. Just as the weeds are collected and burned up with fire, so will it be at the end of the age. The Son of Man will send his angels, and they will collect out of his kingdom all causes of sin and all evildoers.

Chapter Fourteen

The Resurrection

Q. What do the scriptures say about the resurrection of the dead?

A. *Acts 24:15*. I have a hope in God—a hope that they themselves also accept—that there will be a resurrection of both the righteous and the unrighteous.

Q. In what respect shall the resurrection of the good be different from that of the bad?

A. *John 5:28-29*. Do not be astonished at this; for the hour is coming when all who are in their graves will hear his voice and will come out—those who have done good, to the resurrection of life, and those who have done evil, to the resurrection of condemnation.

2 Pet. 3:7. But by the same word the present heavens and earth have been reserved for fire, being kept until the day of judgment and destruction of the Godless.

Q. What is the answer to those who ask how the dead are to be raised? And with what kind of body?

A. *1 Cor. 15:36-44*. Fool! What you sow does not come to life unless it dies. And as for what you sow, you do not sow the body that is to be, but a bare seed, perhaps of wheat or of some other grain. But God gives it a body as he has chosen, and to each kind of seed its own body. Not all flesh is alike, but there is one flesh for human beings, another for animals, another for birds, and another for fish. There are both heavenly bodies and earthly bodies, but the glory of the heavenly is one thing, and that of the earthly is another. There is one glory of the sun, and another glory of the moon, and another glory of the stars, indeed star differs from star in glory. So it is with the resurrection of the dead. What is sown is perishable, what is raised is imperishable. It is sown in dishonor, it is raised in glory. It is sown in weakness, it is raised in power. It is sown a physical body, it is raised a spiritual body. If there is a physical body, there is also a spiritual body.

Q. The apostle seems to be very positive that it is not the natural body, which we now have, in which we shall rise, but a spiritual body!

A. *1 Cor. 15:50-55.* What I am saying, brothers and sisters, is this: flesh and blood cannot inherit the kingdom of God, nor does the perishable inherit the imperishable. Listen, I will tell you a mystery! We will not all die, but we will all be changed, in a moment, in the twinkling of an eye, at the last trumpet. For the trumpet will sound, and the dead will be raised imperishable, and we will be changed. For this perishable body must put on imperishability, and this mortal body must put on immortality. When this perishable body puts on imperishability, and this mortal body puts on immortality, then the saying that is written will be fulfilled: Death has been swallowed up in victory." "Where, O death, is your victory? Where, O death, is your sting?"

A Short Introduction to the Confession of Faith

(Chapter Fifteen)

I have completed the main part of what I promised: to give a full account of our principles in the plain words of scripture. I have also used scripture to answer allegations made against us. So now I summarize our confession of faith. This will be short; there is no need to reiterate every scripture passage already cited in the *Catechism*.

A confession of faith calls for affirming one's faith, rather than refuting objections to it or debating issues about it (more appropriate to a catechism). So that is what I have done here. In order to achieve coherence, it has been necessary occasionally to mix some of my own with scripture words. Likewise, to avoid awkward grammatical construction, I sometimes change the tense and person of verbs. Anyone carefully examining this will find that it has not altered the meaning. For example, where Christ says, "I am the light of the world," nothing is contradicted by changing the first person to the third, and writing, "Christ is the light of the world." Nothing is lost, either, by interchanging nouns and pronouns, i.e., "apostles" for "we." The context sometimes requires this. As any reasonable person can affirm, such alternate words and transitional phrases do not add to the meaning. To avoid petty criticism, the biblical texts that I have excerpted and collated are footnoted. I do not think an impartial reader will quibble with such syntactical changes, although there are always persons who, not finding matters of substance to challenge, will engage in pettifogging instead.

[Ed. note. Early editions of *The Confession* put Barclay's words in italics but did not use ellipses to show omissions within the biblical text. To sustain both the flow and continuity of a document using collated verses, we have used neither italics nor ellipses, and have changed person or tense when appropriate to its confessional nature. Any process of textual selection and arrangement to some extent constitutes interpretation. This was the case with Barclay, and to a lesser extent with us through our substitution of the New Revised Standard Version for the King James Version, and our adaptations of the text to fit Barclay's mode of presentation. The footnote citations serve for testing this process against the texts. To facilitate such review, superscript marks, e.g., "a", "b", etc. correlate text entries with footnote references.]

A Confession of Faith in 23 Articles

(Chapter Sixteen)

Article 1: The True and Saving Knowledge of God

There is one God[a] who is spirit.[b] This is the message the apostles heard from him and proclaim to believers, that God is light and in him there is no darkness at all.[c] There are three that testify: the Father, the Word, and the Holy Spirit, and these three agree [see below[117]]. The Father is in the Son and the Son in the Father. No one knows who the Son is except the Father, and who the Father is except the Son and anyone to whom the Son chooses to reveal him.[d] The Spirit searches everything, even the depths of God. For what human being knows what is truly human except the human spirit that is within? So also no one comprehends what is truly God's except the Spirit of God. Now believers have received not the spirit of the world, but the Spirit that is from God, so that they may understand the gifts bestowed by God.[e] For the Advocate, the Holy Spirit, whom the Father sends in Christ's name, teaches everything, and reminds them of what Jesus said.[f][118]

---

[117] Regarding 1 John 5:7, Barclay included verse 7, here cited in the New King James Version. The New Revised Standard and other versions have deleted this verse because it does not appear in the earliest manuscripts. Consequently in them verse seven reads what in the King James Version is verse eight: "And there are three that bear witness on earth: the Spirit, the water, and the blood, and these three agree as one." John's epistle shows that the reality of Creation (water) and the reality of Redemption (blood) are confirmed by and conform to the reality of the Spirit. Barclay was concerned to show the pivotal role of Christ as the Word, known inwardly and revealed outwardly.

[118] Excerpted from these Scriptures: [a]Eph. 4:6; 1 Cor. 8:4, 6. [b]John 4:24. [c]1 John 1:5. [d]John 10:38b, 14:10-11, 5:26; Matt. 11:27; Luke 10:22. [e]1 Cor. 2:10, 11-12. [f]John 14:26.

Article 2: The Guide and Rule for Christians

Christ asked the Father, who gave believers another Advocate, to be with them forever. This is the Spirit of truth, whom the world cannot receive, because it neither sees him nor knows him. But believers know him, because he abides with them, and dwells in them.[a] Anyone who does not have the Spirit of Christ does not belong to him. For all who are led by the Spirit of God are children of God.[b] This is the covenant God made with the house of Israel to put his laws in their minds, and write them on their hearts, to teach them himself.[c] And the anointing we have received from God abides. We do not need anyone to teach us, because his anointing teaches us about all things, and is true and is not a lie.[d] [119]

Article 3: The Scriptures

Whatever was written in former days was written for our instruction, so that by steadfastness and by the encouragement of the scriptures we might have hope.[a] The sacred writings are able to instruct us for salvation through faith in Christ Jesus. All scripture is inspired by God and is useful for teaching, for reproof, for correction, and for training in righteousness, so that everyone who belongs to God may be proficient, equipped for every good work.[b] No prophecy of scripture is a matter of one's own interpretation, because no prophecy ever came by human will, but men and women moved by the Holy Spirit spoke from God.[c] [120]

Article 4: The Divinity and Pre-existence of Christ

In the beginning was the Word, and the Word was with God, and the Word was God. He was in the beginning with God. All things came into being through him, and without him not one thing came into being.[a] What has come into being is from of old, from ancient days,[b] to make everyone see what is the plan of the mystery hidden for ages in God who created all things.[c] Though he was in the form of God, Christ did not regard equality with God as something to be exploited.[d] He is named Wonderful Counselor, Mighty God, Everlasting Father, Prince of Peace.[e] He is the image of the

---

[119] [a]John 14:16-17. [b]Rom. 8:9, 14. [c]Hebr. 8:10-11. [d]1 John 2:27.
[120] [a]Rom. 15:4. [b]2 Tim. 3:15-17. [c]2 Pet. 1:20-21.

invisible God, the firstborn of all creation.ᶠ Christ is the reflection of God's glory and the exact imprint of God's very being.ᵍ He is clothed in a robe dipped in blood, and his name is called The Word of God.ʰ For in him the whole fullness of deity dwells bodily. In Christ are hidden all the treasures of wisdom and knowledge.ⁱ [121]

Article 5: Christ's Earthly Appearance

The Word became flesh.ᵃ For it is clear that he did not come to help angels, but the descendants of Abraham. He had to become like his brothers and sisters in every respect.ᵇ For we do not have a high priest who is unable to sympathize with our weaknesses, but we have one who in every respect has been tested as we are, yet without sin.ᶜ Christ died for our sins in accordance with the scriptures, was buried, and he was raised on the third day in accordance with the scriptures.ᵈ [122]

Article 6: The Purpose of the Christ's Earthly Appearance

God sent his own Son in the likeness of sinful flesh, and to deal with sin, he condemned sin in the flesh.ᵃ The Son of God was revealed for this purpose, to destroy the works of the devil.ᵇ You know that he was revealed to take away sins.ᶜ Christ gave himself up for us, a fragrant offering and sacrifice to God.ᵈ Through the eternal Spirit he offered himself without blemish to God, to purify our conscience from dead works to worship the living God!ᵉ Christ is the lamb slaughtered from the foundation of the world.ᶠ Our ancestors drank from the spiritual rock that followed them, and the rock was Christ.ᵍ Christ also suffered for us, leaving us an example, so that we should follow in his steps.ʰ For we are to carry in our bodies the death of Jesus, so that the life of Jesus may also be made visible in our bodies. For while we live, we are always being given up to death for Jesus' sake, so that the life of Jesus may be made visible in our mortal flesh.ⁱ And so we know Christ and the power of his resurrection and the sharing of his sufferings by becoming like him in his death.ʲ [123]

---

[121] ᵃJohn 1:1-3. ᵇMicah 5:2b. ᶜEph. 3:9. ᵈPhil. 2:6. ᵉIsa. 9:6b-7a. ᶠCol. 1:15. ᵍHebr. 1:3. ʰRev. 19:13. ⁱCol. 2:9, 3.

[122] ᵃJohn 1:14. ᵇHebr. 2:16-17. ᶜHebr. 4:15. ᵈ1 Cor. 15:3b-4.

[123] ᵃRom. 8:3. ᵇ1 John 3:8b. ᶜ1 John 3:5a. ᵈEph. 5:2. ᵉHebr. 9:12,14b. ᶠRev. 5:8, 12; 13:8. ᵍ1 Cor. 10:1, 4. ʰ1 Pet. 2:21b. ⁱ2 Cor. 4:10, 11. ʲPhil. 3:10.

Article 7: Christ Inwardly Received

God promises to dwell with those who are contrite and humble in spirit.[a] For God has said he will live in them and walk among them.[b] Christ stands at the door, knocking; if we hear his voice and open the door, he will come in and eat with us, and we with him.[c] We should examine ourselves, then, to test whether we are living in the faith, whether Jesus Christ is in us — unless, indeed, we fail the test![d] How great, then, are the riches of the glory of this mystery, which is Christ in us, the hope of glory![e] [124]

Article 8: The New Birth

No one can see the kingdom of God without being born from above.[a] Accordingly we must put away our former way of life…and be renewed in the spirit of our minds, clothing ourselves with the new self, created according to the likeness of God in true righteousness and holiness….This new self is being renewed in knowledge according to the image of our creator.[b] From now on, therefore, we regard no one from a human point of view; even though we once knew Christ from a human point of view, we know him no longer in that way. So if anyone is in Christ, there is a new creation: everything old has passed away; see, everything has become new![c] So, we put on the Lord Jesus Christ[d] and are renewed in the spirit of our minds.[e] For as many of us as were baptized into Christ have clothed ourselves with Christ.[f] We have been born anew, not of perishable but of imperishable seed, through the living and enduring word of God.[g] We boast of nothing except the cross of our Lord Jesus Christ, by which the world has been crucified to us, and us to the world. For in Christ Jesus neither circumcision nor uncircumcision is anything; but a new creation is everything![h] [125]

Article 9: The Unity of Christian Believers

The one who sanctifies and those who are sanctified all have one Father.[a] Thus God has given us precious and very great promises, so that through them we may escape from the corruption that is in the world because of lust, and may become participants of the divine nature.[b] For this reason Jesus prayed that believers may all be one, as the Father is in him and he in

---

[124] [a]Isa. 57:15b. [b]2 Cor. 6:16. [c]Rev. 3:20. [d]2 Cor. 13:5. [e]Col. 1:27.

[125] [a]John 3:3b. [b]Eph. 4:22a-24; Col. 3:10. [c]2 Cor. 5:16-17. [d]Rom. 13:14. [e]Eph. 4:23. [f]Gal. 3:27. [g]1 Pet. 1:23. [h]Gal. 6:14-15.

the Father, and that believers might be one with the Father and Son, and that the glory the Father bestowed upon the Son may be given us, so that they may be one, as the Father and Son are.[c] [126]

Article 10: God's Universal Love and Grace

God so loved the world that he gave his only Son, so that everyone who believes in him may not perish but may have eternal life.[a] God's love was revealed among us in this way: God sent his only Son into the world so that we might live through him. So that if we sin, we have an advocate with the Father, Jesus Christ the righteous; and he is the atoning sacrifice for our sins, and not for ours only but also for the sins of the whole world.[b] By the grace of God Jesus has tasted death for everyone[c] and that he gave himself a ransom for all was attested at the right time. Desiring everyone to be saved and to come to the knowledge of the truth,[d] the Lord is not wanting any to perish, but all to come to repentance.[e] For God did not send the Son into the world to condemn the world, but in order that the world might be saved through him.[f] Christ came as light into the world, so that everyone who believes should not remain in the darkness.[g] Therefore just as one man's trespass led to condemnation for all, so one man's act of righteousness leads to justification and life for all.[h] [127]

Article 11: The Light That Enlightens Everyone

The gospel has been proclaimed to every creature under heaven,[a] which gospel is the power of God for salvation to everyone who has faith,[b] and if our gospel is veiled, it is veiled to those who are perishing. In their case the god of this world has blinded the minds of the unbelievers, to keep them from seeing the light of the gospel of the glory of Christ.[c] And this is the judgment, that the light has come into the world, and people love darkness rather than light because their deeds are evil.[d] This is the true light, which enlightens everyone, coming into the world,[e] by which the unfruitful works of darkness are exposed (for everything exposed by the light becomes visible).[f] For all who do evil hate the light and do not come to the light, so that their deeds may not be exposed.[g] But those who do what is true come to the

---

[126] [a]Hebr. 2:11a. [b]2 Pet. 1:4a. [c]John 17:21a, 22, 23a.

[127] [a]John 3:16. [b]1 John 4:9; 1 John 2:1-2. [c]Hebr. 2:9. [d]1 Tim. 2:6, 4. [e]2 Pet. 3:9. [f]John 3:17. [g]John 12:46. [h]Rom. 5:18.

light, so that it may be clearly seen that their deeds have been done in God. But if we walk in the light as he himself is in the light, we have fellowship with one another, and the blood of Jesus his Son cleanses us from all sin.[h] Therefore we ought to believe in the light, so that we may become children of light.[i] Therefore, today, if we hear his voice, let us not harden our hearts.[j] For Christ wept over Jerusalem, saying "If you, even you, had only recognized on this day the things that make for peace! But now they are hidden from your eyes.[k] ...how often have I desired to gather your children together as a hen gathers her brood under her wings, and you were not willing!"[l]

For stiff-necked people, uncircumcised in heart and ears, are forever opposing the Holy Spirit,[m] as are those who rebel against the light.[n] Therefore, God's Spirit shall not abide in mortals forever,[o] for the wrath of God is revealed from heaven against all ungodliness and wickedness of those who by their wickedness suppress the truth. For what can be known about God is plain to them, because God has shown it to them.[p] To each is given the manifestation of the Spirit for the common good.[q] For the grace of God has appeared, bringing salvation to all, training us to renounce impiety and worldly passions, and in the present age to live lives that are self-controlled, upright, and Godly.[r] This message of grace is able to build us up and to give us the inheritance among all who are sanctified.[s] Indeed, the word of God is living and active, sharper than any two-edged sword, piercing until it divides soul from spirit, joints from marrow; it is able to judge the thoughts and intentions of the heart.[t] So we have the prophetic message more fully confirmed. We do well to be attentive to this as to a lamp shining in a dark place, until the day dawns and the morning star rises in our hearts.[u] This light is nearby, "on our lips and in our heart" that is, the word of faith that we proclaim.[v] For God who said, "Let light shine out of darkness," has shone in our hearts to give the light of the knowledge of the glory of God in the face of Jesus Christ. But we have this treasure in clay jars, so that it may be made clear that this extraordinary power belongs to God and does not come from us.[w] For, as Jesus said, the kingdom of God is not something that can be observed, it is among you.[x] [128]

---

[128] [a]Col. 1:23a. [b]Rom. 1:16. [c]2 Cor. 4:3-4. [d]John 3:19. [e]John 1:9. [f]Eph. 5:11, 13. [g]John 3:20-21. [h]1 John 1:7. [i]John 12:36. [j]Hebr. 4:7. [k]Luke 19:42. [l]Matt. 23:37b. [m]Acts 7:51. [n]Job 24:13. [o]Gen. 6:3. [p]Rom. 1:18, 19. [q]1 Cor. 12:7. [r]Titus 2:11-12. [s]Acts 20:32b. [t]Hebr. 4:12. [u]2 Pet. 1:19. [v]Rom. 10:8. [w]2 Cor. 4:6-7. [x]Luke 17:20-21 (alternate text: "within you").

Article 12: Faith and Justification

Faith is the assurance of things hoped for, the conviction of things not seen. Without faith it is impossible to please God.ᵃ [For justification] the only thing that counts is faith working through love.ᵇ For faith without works being dead, is brought to completion by works.ᶜ For no human being will be justified by the law.ᵈ We are saved, not because of any works of righteousness that we have done, but according to his mercy, through the water of rebirth and renewal by the Holy Spirit.ᵉ We are washed, sanctified, and justified in the name of the Lord Jesus Christ and in the Spirit of our God.ᶠ ¹²⁹

Article 13: Good Works

If we live according to the flesh, we will die; but if by the Spirit we put to death the deeds of the body, we will live.ᵃ For those who have come to believe in God will be careful to devote themselves to good works.ᵇ For God will repay according to each one's deeds, to those who by patiently doing good seek for glory and honor and immortality. This is evidence of the righteous judgment of God to those who by patiently doing good seek for glory and honor and immortality he will give eternal life.ᶜ This is intended to make us worthy of the kingdom of God.ᵈ We must not, therefore, abandon that confidence; it brings a great reward.ᵉ Blessed, then, are those who wash their robes so that they will have the right to the tree of life and may enter the city by the gates.ᶠ ¹³⁰

Article 14: Perfection

Sin will have no dominion over those who are not under law but under grace.ᵃ There is therefore now no condemnation for those who are in Christ Jesus, who walk not according to the flesh but according to the Spirit. For the law of the Spirit of life in Christ Jesus has set us free from the law of sin and of death.ᵇ How can we who died to sin go on living in it? Having been

---

¹²⁹ ᵃHebr. 11:1, 6. ᵇGal. 5:6b. ᶜJames 2:26, 22. ᵈRom. 3:20. ᵉTitus 3:5. ᶠ1 Cor. 6:11.

¹³⁰ ᵃRom. 8:13. ᵇTitus 3:8 ᶜRom. 2:6-7. ᵈ2 Thess. 1:5b. ᵉHebr. 10:35. ᶠRev. 22:14. In KJV, the phrase reads, "who do his commandments." The metaphor suggests faithfulness.

set free from sin we have become slaves of righteousness.[c] We are to be perfect, therefore, as our heavenly Father is perfect.[d] For the yoke of Christ is easy, and his burden is light.[e] And his commandments are not burdensome.[f] Whoever would enter into life must keep the commandments, and we may be sure that we know him, if we obey his commandments. Whoever says, "I have come to know him," but does not obey his commandments, is a liar, and in such a person the truth does not exist. Whoever says, "I abide in him," ought to walk just as he walked.[g] No one who abides in him sins; no one who sins has either seen him or known him. Let no one deceive us; everyone who does what is right is righteous, just as he is righteous. Everyone who commits sin is a child of the devil. Those who have been born of God do not sin, because God's seed abides in them; they cannot sin, because they have been born of God.[h] Not everyone who says "Lord, Lord," will enter the kingdom of heaven, but only the one who does the will of the Father.[i] Circumcision is nothing, and uncircumcision is nothing; but obeying the commandments of God is everything.[j] [131]

Article 15: Perseverance and Falling from Grace

We should be eager to confirm our call and election, for if we do this, we will never stumble.[a] Paul was even willing to punish his body and enslave it, so that after proclaiming the Gospel to others he should not be disqualified.[b] We must take care that none of us may have an evil, unbelieving heart that turns away from the living God.[c] Let us therefore make every effort to enter that rest, so that no one may fall through such disobedience.[d] For it is impossible to restore again to repentance those who have once been enlightened, and have tasted the heavenly gift, and have shared in the Holy Spirit, and have tasted the goodness of the word of God and the powers of the age to come, and then have fallen away.[e] Whoever does not abide in Christ is thrown away like a branch and withers,[f] yet those of us who conquer are

---

[131] [a]Rom. 6:14. [b]Rom. 8:1-2. [c]Rom. 6:18. [d]Matt. 5:48. [e]Matt. 11:30. [f]1 John 5:3b. [g]Matt. 19:17b; 1 John 2:3, 4, 6. [h]1 John 3:6-9. [i]Matt. 7:21. [j]1 Cor. 7:19.

made pillars in the temple of God and will never go out of it.[g] For we are convinced that *nothing* will be able to separate us from the love of God in Christ Jesus our Lord.[h] [132]

Article 16: The Church and Ministry

The church of the living God is the pillar and bulwark of the truth.[a] Christ is the head[b] from whom the whole body, nourished and held together by its ligaments and sinews, grows with a growth that is from God.[c] It is composed of those who are sanctified in Christ Jesus.[d] When Christ ascended on high he gave gifts to his people. The gifts he gave were that some would be apostles, some prophets, some evangelists, some pastors and teachers, to equip the saints for the work of ministry.[e] A leader should be above reproach, respectable, an apt teacher, not a drunkard, not violent but gentle, not quarrelsome, and not a lover of money,[f] hospitable, a lover of goodness, prudent, upright, devout, and self-controlled. Such leaders must have a firm grasp of the word that is trustworthy in accordance with the teaching, so that they may be able both to preach with sound doctrine and to refute those who contradict it.[g] Elders must keep watch over themselves and over all the flock, of which the Holy Spirit has made them overseers, to shepherd the church of God[h] to tend the flock of God that is in their charge, exercising the oversight, not under compulsion but willingly, as God would have us do it—not for sordid gain but eagerly, not lording it over but being examples to the flock.[i] Such elders who rule well are to be considered worthy of double honor, especially those who labor in preaching and teaching.[j] We brothers and sisters are to respect those who labor among us.[k] We are to serve one another with whatever gift each has received. Whoever speaks must do so as one speaking the very words of God; whoever speaks must do so with the strength that God supplies,[l] proclaiming the gospel, not with eloquent wisdom, so that the cross of Christ might not be emptied of its

---

[132] [a]2 Pet. 1:10b. [b]1 Cor. 9:27. [c]Hebr. 3:12. [d]Hebr. 4:11. [e]Hebr. 6:4-6a. [f]John 15:6. [g]Rev. 3:12a. [h]Rom. 8:38-39. [Ed. note: Barclay's "*nothing*" (italics ours) encompasses a wide list of obstacles which Paul listed. Barclay enumerated these in the *Catechism* (chap. 8) but not in the *Confession*. They read: "neither death, nor life, nor angels, nor rulers, nor things present, nor things to come, nor powers, nor height, nor depth, nor anything else in all creation."] Quakers, like other Christians, have had occasion to confirm the abiding love of God through such personal and social testing.

power,ᵐ not with plausible words of wisdom, but with a demonstration of the Spirit and of power. This is so our faith might rest not on human wisdom but on the power of God.ⁿ Yet among the mature we do speak wisdom, though it is not a wisdom of this age or of the rulers of this age, who are doomed to perish. But we speak God's wisdom, secret and hidden, which God decreed before the ages for our glory. And we speak of these things in words not taught by human wisdom but taught by the Spirit.ᵒ For it is not we who speak, but the Spirit of our Father speaking through us.ᵖ

If ministers have sown spiritual good is it too much if they reap our material benefits? The Lord commanded that those who proclaim the gospel should get their living by the gospel. For it is written in the law of Moses, "You shall not muzzle an ox while it is treading out the grain,"ᵠ and as Jesus said, "the laborer deserves to be paid."ʳ An obligation is laid on them, and woe to them if they do not proclaim the gospel! They are entrusted with a commission. What then is their reward? Just this: that in their proclamation they make the gospel free of charge,ˢ coveting no one's silver or gold or clothing. The apostle Paul worked with his own hands to support himself and his companions. We remember the words of Jesus: "It is more blessed to give than to receive."ᵗ

Ministers are not to be like dogs that never have enough. Or like shepherds turned to their own gain,ᵘ feeding themselves and not the Master's sheep.ᵛ They must not be like the prophets who lead God's people astray, who cry "Peace" when they have something to eat, but declare war against those who put nothing into their mouths. Who give judgment for a bribe and teach for a price, who offer oracles for money.ʷ Such false ministers must be silenced, since they are upsetting whole families by teaching for sordid gain what it is not right to teach.ˣ They have left the straight road and have gone astray, following the road of Balaam son of Bosor, who loved the wages of doing wrong. And in their greed they will exploit us with deceptive words.ʸ They are depraved in mind and bereft of the truth, imagining that Godliness is a means of gain. True ministers know, of course, that there is great gain in Godliness combined with contentment; and having food and clothing, will be content.ᶻ [133]

---

[133] ᵃ1 Tim. 3:15b. ᵇCol. 1:18a. ᶜCol. 2:19. ᵈ1 Cor. 1:2. ᵉEph. 4:9, 11, 12. ᶠ1 Tim. 3:2a-3. ᵍTitus 1:8:9. ʰActs 20:28. ⁱ1 Pet. 5:2-3. ʲ1Tim. 5:17. ᵏ1 Thess. 5:12. ˡ1 Pet. 4:10-11a. ᵐ1 Cor. 1:17b. ⁿ1 Cor. 2:4-5. ᵒ1 Cor. 2:6, 7, 13. ᵖMatt. 10:20. ᵠ1Cor. 9:11, 14, 9, 16b. ʳLuke 10:7. ˢ1Cor. 9:17b, 18. ᵗActs 20:33-35. ᵘIsa. 56:11. ᵛEzek. 34:8b. ʷMicah 3:5, 11. ˣTitus 1:11. ʸ2 Pet. 2:15, 3. ᶻ1 Tim. 6:5, 6, 8.

Article 17: Worship

The hour has come, and is now here, when the true worshipers will worship the Father in spirit and truth, for the Father seeks such as these to worship him. God is spirit, and those who worship him must worship in spirit and truth.[a] For the Lord is near to all who call on him, to all who call on him in truth.[b] The Lord is far from the wicked, but he hears the prayer of the righteous.[c] And this is the boldness we have in him, that if we ask anything according to his will, he hears us.[d] What will we do then? We will pray with the spirit, but with the mind also.[e] The Spirit helps us in our weakness; for we do not know how to pray as we ought, but that very Spirit intercedes with sighs too deep for words. And God, who searches the heart, knows what is the mind of the Spirit, because the Spirit intercedes for us according to the will of God.[f] [134]

Article 18: Baptism

As there is one Lord and one faith, there is one baptism,[a] which now saves us—not as a removal of dirt from the body, but as an appeal to God for a good conscience, through the resurrection of Jesus Christ.[b] For John indeed baptized with water but Christ with the Holy Spirit and fire.[c] All of us who have been baptized into Christ Jesus were baptized into his death and are buried with him by baptism into death, so that, just as Christ was raised from the dead by the glory of the Father, so we too might walk in newness of life,[d] having clothed ourselves with Christ.[e] [135]

Article 19: Rituals

The Lord Jesus on the night when he was betrayed took a loaf of bread, and when he had given thanks, he broke it and said, "This is my body that is for you. Do this in remembrance of me." In the same way he took the cup also, after supper, saying, "This cup is the new covenant in my blood. Do this, as often as you drink it, in remembrance of me." For as often as you eat this bread and drink the cup, you proclaim the Lord's death until he comes.[a] And Jesus, knowing that the Father had given all things into his hands, and

---

[134] [a]John 4:23-24. [b]Psalm 145:18. [c]Prov. 15:29. [d]1 John 5:14. [e]1 Cor. 14:15. [f]Rom. 8:26-27.

[135] [a]Eph. 4:5. [b]1 Pet. 3:21. [c]Matt. 3:11. [d]Rom. 6:3-4. [e]Gal. 3:27b.

that he had come from God and was going to God, got up from the table, took off his outer robe, and tied a towel around himself. Then he poured water into a basin and began to wash the disciples' feet and to wipe them with the towel that was tied around him. After he had washed their feet, had put on his robe, and had returned to the table, he said to them, "Do you know what I have done to you? You call me Teacher and Lord—and you are right, for that is what I am. So if I, your Lord and Teacher, have washed your feet, you also ought to wash one another's feet. For I have set you an example, that you also should do as I have done to you."[b]

It seemed good to the Holy Spirit to impose on the early church no further burden than these essentials: to abstain from what has been sacrificed to idols and from blood and from what is strangled and from fornication. If you keep yourselves from these, you will do well.[c] Are any among you sick? They should call for the elders of the church and have them pray over them, anointing them with oil.[d] [136]

Article 20: Christian Liberty about Rituals

The kingdom of God is not food and drink but righteousness and peace and joy in the Holy Spirit.[a] Therefore do not let anyone condemn us in matters of food and drink or of observing festivals, new moons, or Sabbaths. If with Christ we have died to the elemental spirits of the universe, why live as if we still belonged to the world? Why do we submit to regulations, e.g., "Do not handle. Do not taste. Do not touch"? All these regulations refer to things that perish with use; they are simply human commands and teachings.[b] Now that we have come to know God, or rather to be known by God, how can we turn back again to the weak and beggarly elemental spirits to be enslaved to them again? To observing special days, and months, and seasons, and years? The apostle Paul would think his work had been wasted.[c] Some judge one day to be better than another, while others judge all days to be alike. Let all of us be fully convinced in our own minds. Those who observe the day, observe it in honor of the Lord; while those who abstain, abstain in honor of the Lord and give thanks to God.[d] [137]

---

[136] [a]1 Cor. 11:23-26. [b]John 13:3-5, 12-15. [c]Acts 15:28-29. [d]James 5:14.
[137] [a]Rom. 14:17. [b]Col. 2:16, 20, 22. [c]Gal. 4:9-11. [d]Rom. 14:5-6.

Article 21: Oaths, Violence, Persecution

It was said to those of ancient times, "You shall not swear falsely, but carry out the vows you have made to the Lord." But Jesus Christ says to us, "Do not swear at all, either by heaven, for it is the throne of God, or by the earth, for it is his footstool, or by Jerusalem, for it is the city of the great King. And do not swear by your head, for you cannot make one hair white or black.

Let your word be 'Yes, Yes' or 'No, No'; anything more than this comes from the evil one."[a]

And James charges us not to swear, either by heaven or by earth or by any other oath, but let our "Yes" be yes and our "No" be no, so that we may not fall under condemnation.[b] Indeed, we live as human beings, but we do not wage war according to human standards; for the weapons of our warfare are not merely human, but they have divine power to destroy strongholds. We destroy arguments and every proud obstacle raised up against the knowledge of God, and we take every thought captive to obey Christ.[c] Those conflicts and disputes, where do they come from? Do they not come from cravings that are at war within?[d] Christ commands us: "Do not resist an evildoer. But if anyone strikes you on the right cheek, turn the other also."[e] Christians are like lambs in the midst of wolves.[f] They will be hated by all because of Christ.[g] Indeed, all of us who want to live a Godly life in Christ Jesus will be persecuted.[h] Those who are persecuted for righteousness' sake are part of the kingdom of heaven.[i] For if we lose our life for the sake of Christ we will find it.[j] Everyone who acknowledges Christ before others, the Son of Man also will acknowledge before the angels of God.[k] We ought not, therefore, fear those who kill the body but cannot kill the soul; rather fear him who can destroy both soul and body in hell.[l] [138]

Article 22: Christians and Government

Let every person be subject to the governing authorities; for there is no authority except from God, and those authorities that exist have been instituted by God. Therefore whoever resists authority resists what God has appointed, and those who resist will incur judgment. For rulers are not a

---

[138] [a]Matt. 5:33-37. [b]James 5:12. [c]2 Cor. 10:3-5. [d]James 4:1-2. [e]Matt. 5:39. [f]Luke 10:3b. [g]Matt. 10:22. [h]2 Tim. 3:12. [i]Matt. 5:10. [j]Matt. 16:25b. [k]Luke 12:8-9. [l]Matt. 10:28.

terror to good conduct, but to bad. Do we wish to have no fear of the authority? Then we do what is good, and will receive its approval; for it is God's servant for our good. But if we do what is wrong, we should be afraid, for the authority does not bear the sword in vain! It is the servant of God to execute wrath on the wrongdoer. Therefore one must be subject, not only because of wrath but also because of conscience. For the same reason we also pay taxes, for the authorities are God's servants, busy with this very thing. Pay to all what is due them—taxes to whom taxes are due, revenue to whom revenue is due, respect to whom respect is due, honor to whom honor is due.[a] For the Lord's sake we accept the authority of every human institution, whether of the emperor as supreme, or of governors, as sent by him to punish those who do wrong and to praise those who do right. For it is God's will that by doing right we should silence the ignorance of the foolish.[b] Yet it is right in God's sight to listen to him rather than to man. If, for example, we were given strict orders not to teach in Jesus' name we must obey God rather than any human authority.[c] [139]

Article 23: The Resurrection

There will be a resurrection of both the righteous and the unrighteous,[a] those who have done good, to the resurrection of life, and those who have done evil, to the resurrection of condemnation.[b] Flesh and blood cannot inherit the kingdom of God, nor does the perishable inherit the imperishable.[c] And as for what you sow you do not sow the body that is to be, but a bare seed. But God gives it a body as he has chosen, and to each kind of seed its own body. So it is with the resurrection of the dead. What is sown is perishable, what is raised is imperishable. It is sown in dishonor, it is raised in glory. It is sown in weakness, it is raised in power. It is sown a physical body, it is raised a spiritual body.[d] [140]

---

[139] [a]Rom. 13:1-7. [b]1 Pet. 2:13-15. [c]Acts 4:19; 5:28-29.
[140] [a]Acts 24:15b. [b]John 5:29b. [c]1 Cor. 15:50b. [d]1 Cor. 15:37, 38, 42-44a.

A Short Discussion and Appeal to All Christians

(Chapter Seventeen)

I challenge all professing Christians to reason together about what their faith means. Would you take these logical steps? First, subject your *Catechisms* and *Confessions of Faith* to what you consider the basic norm or rule. Second, do not let yourselves be culturally blinded any longer. Third, do not err through ignorance of scriptures or of the power of God. Fourth, freely acknowledge and confess that glorious Gospel and the Light (Jesus Christ) to which the scriptures so clearly witness. Fifth, let your experience corroborate the Gospel witness.

Such reasoning surely leads to an affirmation of doctrines truly derivative from universal principles. These doctrines demonstrate how the love of God is graciously displayed to everyone. Like twins, God's justice and mercy are harmonious. Mercy comes in the continual bestowal of love to all who struggle to follow the Light in their times of visitation. Justice arises in the destruction and cutting away of the sinful natures of those who accept redemption through God's judgments. Justice advances too in the complete overthrow of those who rebel against the Light and, spurning grace, angrily despise spiritual reformation.

Such principles are fundamental to the real and inward justification of faithful believers. Through the life and power of Jesus revealed within, they experience full and complete redemption from the body of death and sin and grow steadily under the influence of God's grace. They must, however, continue to watch lest, lulled into a false sense of security, they depart from and make shipwreck of their hitherto strong faith, searing their conscience in the process. All aspects of the doctrine of Christ lie linked together like a golden chain, giving clear evidence of the certainty and virtue of truth above all heresy, error and deceit, however cunningly gilded with deception. For truth is whole and consistent in all its parts, without dissonance. Truth is wonderfully coherent! It is notably harmonious, eliciting resonance like strings of a well-tuned instrument. In contrast, the principles of certain groups of believers, though approaching truth and acknowledging aspects of it, in many ways stray from it through contradiction and dissonance. Although they allege scriptural support for some of their principles, these Christians strain the interpretation of, or in some cases actually deny, the scriptures.

I make a reasoned appeal to all believers: avoid trying to prove just one or two points by scripture. There are, after all, some generally agreed-upon notions of truth which must be applied to the whole body of beliefs and to its related parts in context. (Dredging up a few texts doesn't suffice.) Of the many *Catechisms* and *Confessions of Faith* by professing Christians I find none, except for the dispensation of faith now revealed, that does not differ greatly from, or contradict, the plain text and clear import of scripture.

Currently, certain people unattached to organized faith are attempting to provide a plausible account of reality. Although they claim a general love for all, they find fault with some part of every account by others, and they give no account of their own religion, because, in the final analysis, most of them have none. In sum: such persons may acknowledge general truths, they may hold to the letter of scripture sufficiently to criticize others; but they do not commit themselves to practicing these general principles. Instead they blame others for neglecting them.

When weighed, such efforts are not sufficient to advance matters of Christian faith. It is not enough to acknowledge many disparate truths while witnessing against error, and yet fail to acknowledge essentials. Because these people cannot give account of their faith in respect to foundational beliefs, what truths they do acknowledge become contradicted. Such critics remain silent in time of trial, unwilling to suffer, adroitly shunning the difficulties persecution lays upon other Christians, whom they refuse to join. This doesn't jibe with their protestations of love for all believers. They want the benefits of Christian faith but not its burdens. This renders suspect their claims to be scriptural. So much for the "stragglers in religion." I return to an assessment of the different Christian sects.

I begin with the most numerous one: the *Roman Catholic*. I can be brief, because Roman Catholics do not presume to prove all their dogmas by scripture. One of their chief doctrines is that of tradition. For them tradition may authenticate doctrines without any scriptural authority. Indeed, the Council of Constance boldly commanded things to be believed *Non obstanta scriptura* ("though the scriptures say the contrary"). It was, indeed, their great folly to try to prove their doctrines through scripture, inasmuch as adoration of saints and images, purgatory, prayers for the dead, the primacy of the bishop of Rome, indulgences, and other things of that sort that have not the least shadow of scriptural support.

Among *Protestants*, I know the *Socinians* allege great respect for the scriptures, exalting them in words as much as others. And yet it is odd to observe how in many ways they are not in agreement with them, and in some key principles quite contrary. For instance, they deny the divinity of Christ, which is as expressly affirmed as any thing can be (*"and the Word was God,"* John 1). They also deny Christ's existence from the beginning against the obvious meaning of John 1 and other Bible texts, as I have shown above in Chapter Three. Other instances could be adduced, but this should be enough to stop their boasting.

The *Arminians* rightly attempt to refute the false doctrine of *absolute reprobation* and to assert *Christ's universal and saving death*. But their efforts fall short, for they do not ground such salvation in that spiritual force that enlightens everyone—the Light of Christ. They assign to natural will and capacity an aspect of that salvation that belongs solely to God's grace and power to initiate, sustain, and accomplish. Along with the *Socinians* and the *Pelagians*, the *Arminians* rightly condemn certain errors, yet they err in not replacing them with truth. Accordingly, they are as justly reproved by the scriptures when they insufficiently account for God's enabling grace as are their adversaries, conversely, for asserting the natural depravity of the human will and its incapacity for good.

On the other hand, it is strange to observe how many *Protestants*, for whom "scripture as the only rule" is the first article in their confessions, in effect deny the universality and sufficiency of Christ's death, contrary to express words of scripture, e.g., "He tasted death for everyone" (Hebrews 2:9). Surely nothing other than universality and sufficiency was intended when the writer stated "For the grace of God has appeared, bringing salvation to all" (Titus 2:11). Other scriptures could be adduced to reinforce this point. Similar things could be said about the *Protestant* denial of the perfection of the saints, and their asserting the impossibility of falling away from an initial experience of true and saving grace. Such assertions are contrary to scriptures, as has been noted in previous chapters. To reveal how the devil has deceived many under a pretense of wisdom, leading them to cloak with scripture false and harmful doctrine, in the next chapter I lift examples from that *Confession of Faith* and *Catechism* crafted by the so-called Westminster theologians. It is, after all, not only the most widely accepted doctrinal statement for the people of Britain and Ireland but also the stated faith for churches in France, the Netherlands, and elsewhere. I will show what erroneous principles—and their consequences—occur when the certain and direct meanings of scriptural words are disregarded.

A Brief Look at Scriptural Proofs of Selected Articles in the Westminster Confession of Faith

(Chapter Eighteen)

It is my purpose here to examine only two or three articles of the Westminster Confession, as examples the reader may apply similar analysis to the rest if desired.

In the first chapter, section 1, where two things are asserted: First *That God has committed his will now wholly to writing.* Second, *That the former ways of God's revealing his will, as by immediate revelation, have now ceased.* Consider the scriptures alleged for proof of the first assertion. These are the texts they have chosen:

Prov. 22:19-21. So that your trust may be in the Lord, I have made them known to you today—yes, to you. Have I not written for you thirty sayings of admonition and knowledge, to show you what is right and true?

Luke 1:3-4. I too decided, after investigating everything carefully from the very first, to write an orderly account for you, most excellent Theophilus, so that you may know the truth concerning the things about which you have been instructed.

Rom. 15:4. For whatever was written in former days was written for our instruction, so that by steadfastness and by the encouragement of the scriptures we might have hope.

Matt. 4:4, 7, 10. But he answered, "It is written, 'One does not live by bread alone, but by every word that comes from the mouth of God.'" ...Jesus said to him, "Again it is written, 'Do not put the Lord your God to the test.'" ...Jesus said to him, "Away with you, Satan! for it is written, 'Worship the Lord your God, and serve only him.'"

Isa. 8:19, 20. Now if people say to you, "Consult the ghosts and the familiar spirits that chirp and mutter; should not a people consult their Gods, the dead on behalf of the living, for teaching and for instruction?" Surely, those who speak like this will have no dawn!

Isn't it remarkable that theologians could be so incredulous as to imagine these scriptures support their allegations? Or that people who do not take things merely on trust should be so foolish as to believe them? Although God made known and wrote excellent things to Solomon, although Luke wrote for Theophilus an account of many events in Christ's earthly life, *many other things were never written.* John affirms this: "But there are also many other things that Jesus did; if every one of them were written down, I suppose that the world itself could not contain the books that would be written" (John 21:25). And, "Now Jesus did many other signs in the presence of his disciples, which are not written in this book" (John 20:30).

Although Christ used many scriptures against Satan, and Isaiah directed people to the law and testimonies, who could be so irrational as to claim *it naturally follows from this that God has now committed his will wholly to writing*? Such a conclusion is no more deductible from the scriptures than if I should claim that because the Westminster theologians have asserted many unfounded things nothing they say is founded. Countervailing scripture suggests it is neither sensible nor warranted to infer from a few selected verses *that God had committed his counsel wholly to writing.*

Consider the second doctrine: *that the former ways* [of revelation] *are now ceased.* To support this assertion they adduce the following scriptures:

2 Tim. 3:15. Paul writes to Timothy "...how from childhood you have known the sacred writings that are able to instruct you for salvation through faith in Christ Jesus."[141]

Hebr. 1:1-2. Long ago God spoke to our ancestors in many and various ways by the prophets, but in these last days he has spoken to us by a Son, whom he appointed heir of all things, through whom he also created the worlds.

2 Pet. 1:19. So we have the prophetic message more fully confirmed. You will do well to be attentive to this as to a lamp shining in a dark place, until the day dawns and the morning star rises in your hearts.

These verses prove nothing more than the previous argument. If Paul believed as the Westminster theologians, he would have been caught in a contradiction, for the apostles acknowledged that John's revelation was written long afterwards—"whatever was written in former days" (Rom. 15:4) had continuity with what was yet to be written. As for the Peter quotation (2 Pet. 1:19), it begs the question to assume the Son speaks *only*

---

[141] For some reason 2 Timothy 3:15 did not appear in the 1673 or 1690 editions, but it is found in the 1691 edition. Clearly the text refers to it.

through the scriptures. The citation from the book of Hebrews (1:1-2), far from supporting their contention, actually refutes it! God does indeed now speak to us by his Son, and God's revelation to these biblical writers was inward. We may trust the same apostle better than these current theologians, for he says that as soon as Christ was revealed in him he straightway obeyed (Acts 9:20). He tells us, also, that except Christ be in us, we are reprobates (2 Cor. 13:5). Surely Christ is not speechless (John 16:13), inasmuch as He has promised to indwell us, walk with us, and be with us until the end of the world (Matt. 28:20).

Furthermore, John tells us that an inward anointing is to teach us all things (John 14:26). It is not absolutely essential for some person to teach us. How, then, can revelation have ceased, seeing that God speaks to us by Christ, and Christ must be within us? Surely these Westminster ministers have not interpreted scriptures rightly. They have distorted them—made a wax nose out of them—contrary to their own assertions (section six) that *all things necessary are either expressly set down, or by good and necessary consequences may be deduced.* Other things in this same chapter will not pass the test either, for the scripture proofs alleged are ridiculous, but for the sake of brevity I have omitted them.

Look at Chapter 21, Section 7, where they say that *the Sabbath from the resurrection of Christ was changed into the first day of the week, which in scripture,* say they, *is called the Lord's day, and is to be continued to the end of the world as the Christian Sabbath.* They posit three arguments in support of their contention.

First, that the first day of the week replaces the seventh for a Sabbath. They attempt to prove this by citing 1 Cor. 16:1, 2. "Now concerning the collection for the saints: you should follow the directions I gave to the churches of Galatia. On the first day of every week, each of you is to put aside and save whatever extra you earn, so that collections need not be taken when I come." And, Acts 20:7: "On the first day of the week, when we met to break bread, Paul was holding a discussion with them; since he intended to leave the next day, he continued speaking until midnight."

These are not direct proofs, of course. Furthermore, one cannot deduce a Sabbath replacement from Paul's request for the Corinthians to set aside extras, or because he ate with them and preached until midnight. Such a generalization is more hasty than sound! Express authority for such a major commandment would need to be more substantive than that. The text shows clearly why the disciples met so frequently, and why Paul preached so long: he had to leave the next morning. Nothing is said about a Sabbath.

About their second assertion: *the first day of the week is therefore called the Lord's day*, is drawn, yet more strangely, from Rev. 1:10: "I was in the spirit on the Lord's day, and I heard behind me a loud voice like a trumpet." No particular day of the week is mentioned, so for them to claim John meant the first day is only asserted and not proven.

To support their third assertion: *it is to be continued to the end of the world as the Christian Sabbath*, they cite these scriptures:

Exod. 20:8, 10, 11. Remember the Sabbath day, and keep it holy. Six days you shall labor and do all your work. But the seventh day is a Sabbath to the Lord your God; you shall not do any work—you, your son or your daughter, your male or female slave, your livestock, or the alien resident in your towns. For in six days the Lord made heaven and earth, the sea, and all that is in them, but rested the seventh day; therefore the Lord blessed the Sabbath day and consecrated it.

Isa. 56:2, 4, 6, 7. Happy is the mortal who does this, the one who holds it fast, who keeps the Sabbath, not profaning it, and refrains from doing any evil. For thus says the Lord: To the eunuchs who keep my Sabbaths, who choose the things that please me and hold fast my covenants....And the foreigners who join themselves to the Lord, to minister to him, to love the name of the Lord, and to be his servants, all who keep the Sabbath, and do not profane it, and hold fast my covenant—these I will bring to my holy mountain, and make them joyful in my house of prayer; their burnt offerings and their sacrifices will be accepted on my altar; for my house shall be called a house of prayer for all peoples.

Matt. 5:17, 18. "Do not think that I have come to abolish the law or the prophets; I have come not to abolish but to fulfill. For truly I tell you, until heaven and earth pass away, not one letter, not one stroke of a letter, will pass from the law until all is accomplished.

If these citations prove anything it would be the continuity of the seventh day, because in all the law there is no mention of the first day being a Sabbath. If such a line of argument were considered sound I know of no absurdities so great, no heresies so damnable, no superstitions so ridiculous that they could not be cloaked with the authority of scripture.

In the first several verses of Chapter 27 of the Westminster Confession, *sacraments* are described at some length. But in all the scriptures cited there is not one word about sacraments. And for good reason: there is nothing in the Bible about them. To allege scriptural signification is to beg the question when they have asserted previously that *the whole counsel of God is contained in the scripture.* This does not jibe with their ostensible effort to clear away errors accumulated in the Roman tradition—reformation from which is so much a part of their faith.

In the fourth section they assert two things: first, *that there are only two sacraments under the gospel* and, second, that "these two are baptism and the supper." Here are the scriptures they use in support of their assertions:

Matt. 28:19. Go therefore and make disciples of all nations, baptizing them in the name of the Father and of the Son and of the Holy Spirit,

1 Cor. 11:20, 23. When you come together, it is not really to eat the Lord's supper. For I received from the Lord what I also handed on to you, that the Lord Jesus on the night when he was betrayed took a loaf of bread,

1 Cor. 4:1. Think of us in this way, as servants of Christ and stewards of God's mysteries.

Hebr. 5:4. And one does not presume to take this honor, but takes it only when called by God, just as Aaron was.

Now, granting there were such things as *sacraments* to be so solemnly performed, do these scriptures prove that these and only these two are sacraments? No, there is not the least shadow of proof. Their definition of sacrament in the larger Catechism is this: *"The parts of a sacrament are two, the one an outward and sensible sign, used according to Christ's own appointment; the other, an inward and spiritual grace thereby signified."* Well, foot washing and anointing the sick with oil, among other activities, fit that definition. Put to the test, then, whether by name or number, two, seven, or even seventy, there is no scriptural warrant for ritual sacrament, but only human constructs. And yet how incredible to observe with what great confidence some people allege scriptural authority for doctrines that have no scriptural foundation!

I have focused upon these three: *scriptures, Sabbath, and sacraments,* because these are the issues over which we Quakers are chastised, and criticized for being in error. What we believe about them and how our testimony agrees with scriptures has been demonstrated in preceding chapters. An open minded reader will surely see that, despite their claims, little scriptural proof can be adduced to support the Westminster allegations.

Appendix A
Barclay's original title page

A CATECHISM
AND
CONFESSION OF FAITH

APPROVED OF, AND AGREED UNTO

BY THE

GENERAL ASSEMBLY

OF THE

PATRIARCHS, PROPHETS AND APOSTLES, CHRIST HIMSELF
CHIEF SPEAKER IN AND AMONG THEM

which containeth a true and faithful account of the principles and doctrines, which are most surely believed by the churches of Christ in Great Britain and Ireland, who are reproachfully called by the name of Quakers, yet are found in the one faith with the primitive church and saints, as is most clearly demonstrated by some plain scripture testimonies, without consequences or commentaries, which are here collected, and inserted by way of answer to a few weighty, yet easy and familiar questions, fitted as well for the wisest and largest, as for the weakest and lowest capacities.—To which is added, an Expostulation with, and appeal to, all other Professors.

BY ROBERT BARCLAY

[Editor's note: As a zealous twenty-four-year-old Quaker, chafing under a bureaucratic church hierarchy that persecuted dissenters from the established church, Robert Barclay issued a charismatic (if somewhat satirical) challenge to institutional authority in his original title, which appeared in several eighteenth- and nineteenth-century editions. It is reproduced here in one of its several formats.]

Appendix B

Editorial notes about method and text

A Note on Method

When I proposed doing a modern English version of *Barclay's Catechism and Confession of Faith*, Arthur Roberts enthusiastically offered to work with me. It soon became clear that not only the biblical quotations but Barclay's text itself needed rephrasing, or in some cases rewriting, if it was not to appear quaint, or even baffling, to readers. The English language has changed considerably over three and a quarter centuries. Furthermore, at many points Barclay's style of writing was ponderous, indirect, or convoluted. Some sentences seemed almost endless!

This rephrased text includes Barclay's Preface, his questions in the Catechism, his Introduction to the Confession, his Discussion with other Christians, and his Examination of scripture proofs used in the Westminster Confession.

Arthur Roberts soon demonstrated a particular gift for turning all this into modern prose, usually of shorter length, and always of greater lucidity. Nearly all this work was done by him, with only minor revisions made at my suggestion.

It was upon strong urging by both Arthur Roberts and Paul Anderson that all Biblical quotations would be those of the New Revised Standard Version of 1989, and an agreement was reached with the National Council of Churches of Christ. I proposed that if we were to standardize the NRSV, then footnotes should cite alternate wording from other recent versions where the meaning could be expressed more clearly or concisely. Inasmuch as this book will likely be used in Christian education classes this mode of presentation should be helpful in promoting discussion.

A Critical Text

How did we establish a critical text? How did later versions compare with the original 1673 text? How faithfully did the many editions of the eighteenth and nineteenth centuries follow Barclay? To answer that I secured the help of the Monmouth County (New Jersey) Library[142] to obtain microfilm

---

[142] I am particularly indebted to Louise Parr, reference librarian at the Wall Township Branch, for help in obtaining these documents.

copies by interlibrary loan of the 1673 original, and the Third Edition of 1690 (the year Barclay died) for comparison. It is remarkable how faithful later Quaker printers were in transmitting Barclay's own words.

In 1690 Robert Barclay himself made several changes. A couple sentences were added to the final paragraph of the Preface, and a Table of Contents was provided. The laborious comparisons proved their worth in showing that the only extensive modifications by Barclay consisted of enlarging Chapter Ten, on worship, by adding a number of questions and answers (sets three through seven) that were not in the 1673 original.

There was one amusing change! In a critique of the Westminster Assembly, to show the illogic of concluding that divine revelation is limited to writing, Barclay used the phrase, "who will *be so mad* as to say." This phrase remained in the 1690, 1691, and 1726 versions. It was later softened to read "who will say." Whoever did the editing evidently thought Barclay's language *was a little too plain*! We have used the word *irrational* in this text. Colloquially, one might say about illogical deductions, "hey, that's crazy!"

We avoided the temptation to omit from Chapter Twelve the numerous scriptural quotations about slavery and the role of women. They have been left intact, but Arthur Roberts prepared extensive yet concise footnotes (#s 98, 100) indicating the seventeenth-century context in which these were interpreted, and the changes in society since then.

—*Dean Freiday*